JIM CARR

A—Z
of
autism

A guide for
parents
and
professionals

Dedicated to all the young people, parents,
carers and professionals who have helped me
research and write this book. Thank you all.

A–Z of autism: A guide for parents and professionals

ISBN: 978-1-85503-623-9

© Jim Carrington 2018
Illustrations by Camille Medina/Beehive Illustration

This edition published 2018
10 9 8 7 6 5 4 3 2 1

Printed in the UK by Page Bros (Norwich) Ltd
Designed and typeset by Andy Wilson for Green Desert Ltd

LDA, 2 Gregory Street, Hyde, Cheshire, SK14 4HR

www.ldalearning.com

is for

Welcome

I realise it's a little unconventional to start an A–Z guide with a W, but it would have been even weirder to stick the Welcome section at the back of the book, wouldn't it?

So, welcome to the parent's A–Z guide of autism. I'm assuming you're here because someone close to you either has autism spectrum condition (ASC), or you suspect they might have.

Before I begin, I should explain that, strictly speaking, I am no 'expert'. I'm not a professor or a doctor. I don't work in a specialist school or autism base. But what I do have, as a Special Educational Needs Coordinator (SENCo) and parent, is a lot of experience of working with children with ASC and their families and other professionals. If I have any expertise, I'm pretty sure that's where it lies. A large proportion of my time is spent explaining ASC and how to deal with the Special Educational Needs (SEN) system. I've spent my working life trying to make things which can be confusing and stressful seem a little plainer and easier to understand. So that's what this book is – a parent's guide to ASC, which is fun to read and easily understood. In writing it, I've tried to draw not only on my own experience, but also on the experiences of many parents, children and teachers. In order to get the theoretical, scientific, statistical and clinical information correct, I've also drawn from a wide range of reliable sources. Many of the things I've written about are things about which our understanding is currently evolving (e.g. possible links between eating disorder and ASC, diagnosing girls with ASC, and pathological demand avoidance (PDA)), but I've tried to make my advice and information as up-to-the-minute as possible.

Welcome to the jungle

If your child has a diagnosis of ASC (or you suspect one might be round the corner), the chances are that you'll be about to enter the world of SEN. A lot of parents refer to the world of SEN as a jungle, and for good reason. Just like being dropped in the jungle, the world of SEN can be a confusing and sometimes scary place. However, if you know where to look there are wonders to be seen. It will be an incredibly tough journey, but one that can be thoroughly rewarding. There will be times when you're forced out of your comfort zone. There will probably be meetings with the tribes from the local authority (LA) or with a team of professionals where it seems like they're speaking in a new and confusing language which seems to consist almost entirely of acronyms like IEP (individual education plan) and PDA and PECS (picture exchange communication system). You'll probably take some paths which turn out to be dead ends. There may be times when you're making very nice progress through the jungle, thank you very much, only for an enormous, hairy, venomous spider to drop down right in front of you, in the form of a service being cut.

> There may be times when you're making very nice progress through the jungle, thank you very much, only for an enormous, hairy, venomous spider to drop down right in front of you, in the form of a service being cut.

The thing about real jungles is that most people who go there are either intrepid explorers who are well trained and well prepared for the journey, or they're locals who know every twig and insect, every twist and turn of the jungle. Usually though, people end up dumped into the SEN jungle unprepared and unexpectedly. In many cases, what they could really do with is a guidebook, which is exactly what this book aims to be. Think of it as a survival guide to the SEN jungle (ASC branch), specifically designed to help you and your family get the best out of the journey.

Inside, you'll find an alphabetised list of the key issues which you may come across as a parent of a child with ASC – all the way from diagnosis to selecting the right school provision for your child. You'll also find some dispatches from the front line, in the form of case studies from parents who've been there, done that and come away with the T-shirt.

I hope you enjoy the book and find plenty of use in it. Normal A–Z orderliness will now resume.

is for

Annual review

Annual review. Two words which strike fear into many parents' hearts.

If your child has an Education, Health and Care Plan (EHCP), they will have an annual review each year, and sometimes – despite the word 'annual' – more often.

So what is an annual review?

An annual review is a meeting where your child's EHCP is discussed and reviewed. As the name suggests, they happen annually, although they can occur every six months in early years. You (and sometimes, if it's appropriate, your child) will be invited. So will all the professionals who work with your child. In some cases, there may also be a representative from the local education authority. In my experience, you rarely get a full complement of professionals at a meeting, but they will have provided advice, regardless of whether they turn up to the meeting or not.

Make sure you turn up. This is your best chance to get *your* voice heard and your questions answered!

Before the meeting

The school Special Educational Needs Coordinator (SENCo) will usually arrange the meeting, sending out letters six weeks before the meeting is due to take place. They'll send a form for you to fill in and return before the meeting, which is focused on the progress your child is making towards the outcomes on their EHCP, and will usually give you a chance to pre-warn them of any matters you would like discussed at the meeting.

The school will usually ask you (and all professionals) to return your forms two weeks prior to the meeting, so they can copy and distribute all the reports and forms to all who will be attending.

What should I do before the meeting?

I'd recommend that you take time to read through the reports that are generated for the review and make sure you understand them. If you don't, get in touch with whoever produced the report and ask them questions. I would also recommend reading back through the EHCP to make sure that it still describes the child that you know and love (you'd be amazed at how often I've read statements of SEN and EHCPs which describe a child who isn't yet out of nappies, when in reality that child is now a strapping ten-year-old, who can look after themselves). Make a note of any changes you'd like to be considered in the EHCP. Also, take some time to go through the outcomes set in Section E. This is usually what the majority of the meeting will focus on – the progress your child has made, and what their next steps are.

What happens at the meeting?

In most cases, the meeting will be chaired by the SENCo from your child's school. They will take everyone through the statement or EHCP section by section, making sure that the information is up to date. This is where having done your prep before the meeting will come in handy – you can ask them to change any details which are incorrect or out of date. When it gets to Section E (outcomes) and Section F (provision), the chair of the meeting will invite everyone present to comment on the progress that your child has made since the last review in relation to each outcome. They'll also use the reports of any invitees who couldn't make the meeting to make sure their views are taken into account. Your child should also have the chance to make their voice heard – this might be in pictorial form, by answering some questions on what they like in school and what they'd like to be done differently, or by attending some of the meeting and speaking themselves. The decision on how to get your child's opinion has to be taken based on the needs of your child. Once a clear idea of progress has been established, the SENCo will invite the attendees to consider the next small-step targets which will help your child towards meeting the outcomes set in the EHCP. Depending on the age of your child, other issues may come up, such as attendance, independent travel, personal budgets, funding and providing extra support or reducing support. The meeting is also a chance for you to check that everything which the EHCP states *should* be happening actually *is* happening.

Okay, that's what's *meant* to happen, but what *actually* happens?

As with everything in the SEN world, there are horror stories of annual reviews, and other stories where everyone lives happily ever after. Your experience of annual reviews may be very different to others'.

A good annual review might be attended by all those invited, who all give their reports in before the deadline, meaning the SENCo can distribute them well before the meeting. The chair might invite you to speak, as well as the professionals. The meeting might focus in on some positives, as well as attempting to resolve any problems. You'll go home proud of your child, confident that their needs are being met.

A bad annual review might not be attended by any of the professionals, except those who work in the educational setting (e.g. the SENCo, teacher, teaching assistant). Many of the reports and forms may not have been received by the chair, meaning they also haven't a chance to be used in the meeting. Most of the discussion will be about what your child can't do. Your views are either not invited, or dismissed. By the time you get home you'll feel utterly defeated and demoralised. While the SEND Code of Practice (2017) states that representatives of the local authority (LA), health professionals and social care professionals *must* be invited, it does not state that they must attend. Likewise, while the Code of Practice states that the educational setting

> A good annual review might be attended by all those invited, who all give their reports in before the deadline, meaning the SENCo can distribute them well before the meeting.

must request reports, it does not state that the professionals must produce them.

If you're lucky enough to get the former type of annual review, count your lucky stars. If it's the latter, make a complaint to your LA and ask for another review to be held, with all the necessary reports. And before the next annual review, consider taking someone with you to the meeting.

What happens after the meeting?

After the meeting, the school will put together all the forms, reports and so on that are generated by the annual review process. If there are any actions which have arisen from the meeting, they should have been set a timescale and a person responsible for doing them. Copies of all the paperwork will go to those invited to the meeting and to the LA's SEN caseworker. If there are any changes which need to take place – to the wording of the EHCP, funding or provision – the caseworker will then get to work. For some things (e.g. changes to provision or funding), they will need to submit the papers to an independent panel who will make the decision on whether to proceed. If a request is turned down, you will receive information about how to appeal the decision.

What is an interim review?

An interim review can be called at any time, usually when there is an issue which urgently needs addressing. For example, an interim review might be called about seeking a change to funding, provision or placement, to name but a few. The process is fairly similar to an annual review, but it might be called at much shorter notice and discussion is usually centred around the specific area of need which has necessitated the meeting, rather than on monitoring the EHCP in general terms.

What is a transition review?

Transition reviews happen when a transition is coming up. The points of transition will be different in different LAs, depending on what type of schools they have. But transition reviews could occur when your child is due to move schools: from an early years setting to a primary school; from an infant to a junior school; from a primary to a middle school; from a primary to a secondary school; from a middle to a secondary school; from a secondary school to a post-16 placement. The meeting is effectively an annual review with a little more tagged on. Someone from the LA should attend the meeting to provide you with information about how to find the right school for your child and how the process will work. They should also give you more information on where to get support in finding the right school place (see page 113 for more on finding the right school provision). More so than at other reviews, the transition reviews tend to be where LAs are keen to make changes to EHCPs to ensure they're bang up to date.

What if my child isn't in a school?

In the case of children who are not in school – perhaps because they are at pre-school, or being home schooled – the LA will be responsible for organising the annual review. For children below five years of age, the annual review may happen more often than annually – perhaps every three or six months.

Asperger syndrome (AS)

Asperger syndrome (pronounced with a hard *g*) is a lifelong condition which is on the autism spectrum. While many people diagnosed before 2013 will have been given a diagnosis of AS, now you're more likely to get diagnosed with ASC (the umbrella term for all autism conditions). However, I know it isn't unknown for the diagnosis team to refer to AS either verbally or in writing in their feedback.

AS describes people who have difficulties in social communication and understanding, but usually have average or above-average intelligence. They often do not have problems with speech, unlike others on the autism spectrum, but may have difficulties understanding or processing language.

The history bit

In 1944, Austrian paediatrician Han Asperger was working with four young patients who appeared to be of average or above-average intellect, who had similar social difficulties. They all lacked empathy, struggled with non-verbal communication and spoke in a stilted or overly formal way. They could be clumsy. They also had narrow interests, which tended to dominate their conversations. Asperger wrote about these cases, but it wasn't until the 1980s, when Lorna Wing published case studies on patients with similar presentations, that the term Asperger syndrome was used, and later added to the criteria used for diagnosing mental disorders.

What does AS look like?

People with AS often show some of the below traits.

- Inappropriate and/or limited social interactions
- Difficulty picking up non-verbal communication, such as gestures and facial expressions
- Average or above-average verbal skills. They can be precocious in speech, but sometimes use words inappropriately
- Difficulty understanding non-literal language
- A lack of eye contact
- Limited and repetitive interests
- Speaking in a monotone, or very loudly
- Discussing self, rather than others
- Awkward movements and mannerisms
- Difficulty understanding emotions (both their own and others')
- Restricted and repetitive patterns of behaviour
- Enjoying spending time alone
- Becoming overwhelmed by gatherings of people and social situations
- A narrow friendship group (i.e. 1 or 2 people)

> Asperger syndrome describes people who have difficulties in social communication and understanding, but usually have average or above-average intelligence.

Hard to spot?

AS sometimes goes unrecognised in children, even right into adulthood. The reason for this is often that, unlike others on the autism spectrum, those with AS are likely to have average or above-average intellect and good language skills. In fact, these language skills can sometimes be precocious, so the child seems to be well above average. This can mean that children with AS are doing well in their learning and there is no cause to question whether they may have a condition. It is often not until they start experiencing difficulties with friendships, anxiety or social situations, that AS or ASC is recognised. It can go unrecognised in girls, as they often present differently to boys (see page 70 for more on girls with ASC).

I know loads of people who fit that description who have no diagnosis. So why is a diagnosis important?

It's true, there will be thousands of people who have gone their whole lives undiagnosed and have suffered no ill effects from it. However, a diagnosis can help someone to understand why they have difficulties with some things. A lot of people with AS report that they've always felt 'different' from other people, but have not known why. My favourite ever description of autism is from Siobhan Dowd's *The London Eye Mystery*, where the main character, Ted, describes himself as having a brain that runs on a 'different operating system' to everyone else's. A diagnosis of AS often helps people to understand this feeling of otherness and to be able to put strategies into place to help them adapt to situations they have previously found difficult.

> AS sometimes goes unrecognised in children, even right into adulthood, because they are likely to have average or above-average intellect and good language skills.

It's very common for those with AS to feel a high degree of anxiety. Having a diagnosis can give access to strategies and treatments that may help them overcome their difficulties and lessen anxiety.

> 66 *My brain runs on a different operating system from other people's. I see things they don't and sometimes they see things I don't.* 99
> London Eye Mystery, Siobhan Dowd

Everyone with AS is a genius, right?

No, although television, the media and fiction often portray AS in this way. Some people with AS might be geniuses, but just because you have AS does not mean you are automatically a genius (see page 67 for more on this topic). However, those with AS can do very well at school, at work and in life. Often, people with AS are able to maintain a single-minded focus on one thing, and therefore develop great depth of knowledge in that area. For some children, that area of special interest might be numbers, and they'll go on to be an ace mathematician. For others, the area of special interest could be a video game.

What helps people with AS?

The greatest area of need is usually in social skills. Things that seem to come naturally to most don't for those with AS. Some of these skills can be taught and practised though. Social stories (see page 136) are often an effective way of doing this, identifying a situation that the individual needs help dealing with and then outlining an appropriate way to respond in that situation in future. For instance, for a child who has difficulty in taking turns, a social story could focus on how this affects others, and what to do while waiting for their turn.

Comic strip conversations (see page 30) are also helpful as a way of understanding what went wrong in a social situation. They focus on the events of a situation as well as the thoughts, feelings and speech of those involved. They can also help to teach a more appropriate way to deal with a similar situation in the future.

Therapies like cognitive behavioural therapy (CBT) (see page 29) can also be helpful for those with AS, as they teach strategies to help manage anxiety more effectively.

CASE STUDY

James

My son, James, was angry and unhappy as a baby: super-sensitive to touch, he screamed and screamed and didn't sleep. He could be violent with other children, attacking them if they got in his way. I had to leave countless playgroups, and many outings were cut short due to his behaviour.

When he was young, his problems were sensory; touch, light and sound could overload him and he would explode into violence or tantrums. Not just in supermarkets – it happened in the child seat on the bike (too much whooshing of air or noise or speed, I guess). He hated the feel of fabrics on his skin and it was a real battle to get him dressed. He didn't wear socks or pants until he was 10. The only things he could tolerate were polyester T-shirts and polyester tracksuit bottoms. I could hardly get a coat on him in the winter and he would literally turn blue with cold rather than wear a coat which was tight on his wrists or felt bad. But at least by then he could explain it – for years before, I just couldn't understand why he wouldn't get dressed.

He had obsessions and played repetitively, utterly focused on a task. At a very young age, he would line up Playmobil® people meticulously, all with a hat on, or with their hair removed, or their arms up or down or at an angle – he paid a huge amount of attention to tiny detail even before the age of two.

He would build a traffic jam on his floor using hundreds of cars and ask me to come and look at it, then change it slightly and ask me if I could tell what had changed. He was a very verbal child, but wouldn't talk about friends or feelings. He also had amazing mathematical ability for a small child: I was teaching him about negative numbers when he was five, because he liked it. He would like to add up at bedtime to calm himself. He was clearly an intelligent child, but hyper-sensitive and unbending in his thinking, inflexible, rigid, unable to adapt to change.

He always had lots of friends – bizarrely, not at all in a bubble or friendless, which is often the stereotype – but he was very authoritarian with them, and they often followed him as he was so bright.

At school he hid under tables and tore up his work. He had help at school because he couldn't cope on his own and at the age of five and a half he was diagnosed with Asperger syndrome. I'd been to the doctor before this, but was only taken seriously when his school confirmed that his behaviour was unusual and they suspected ASC. Before that, the doctors told me it was my parenting style that was to blame. By then I had already adapted my treatment of him, because I had long realised he needed more understanding from me. I had resolved to be on his side long before we finally got any help. I just hugged him and loved him more... and he eventually stopped fighting me and started to just break down and cry and cry and cry.

Changing the way I treated him was the biggest turning point. He started to see I was on his side and he would let me try to help, and he cried and kissed me and just let it all out. One by one, we went through many totally bizarre phases. From one day to the next, he'd move onto a new obsession or phrase he would repeat. But we got through them to the point that he decided he didn't need help any longer – he could do it on his own.

And he really has. He has learnt to moderate his behaviours, although he still has some odd moments. He is still very sensory and touchy-feely, but it's more positive now. He wears normal clothes, doesn't wet the bed, has friends, is very reasonable and quite philosophical. My son still finds it hard to cope with some new situations and likes to know exactly what is going to happen, and when and where and who is going to be there – so there is still some social anxiety – but he tries to cope by asking for all the information he needs to be reassured.

He's 14 now, 15 this year, and he's become someone I am really proud of. He's not recognisable as the angry, violent, furious little child.

Autism spectrum condition (ASC)

ASC stands for autism spectrum condition. It is one of a few different names which mean basically the same thing and tend to be interchangeable – other common ones you'll hear and read are autism spectrum disorder (ASD), autism, the spectrum. Although on most reports you'll find it referred to as ASD, throughout this book I've referred to it as ASC. This is simply because I prefer to think of the many presentations of autism as a condition, rather than a disorder.

> ASC is a neurodevelopmental condition which can affect speech and language development, social communication, social imagination and social interaction.

What is ASC?

ASC is a neurodevelopmental condition which can affect speech and language development, social communication, social imagination and social interaction. It is also common for those with autism to have sensory differences. ASC is a spectrum condition, which means that it encompasses people with many varied and different presentations. No two people with autism are the same and the extent of the difficulties people with ASC present with can be very different – some may be non-verbal, some may have other learning delays, while others may have a few difficulties with social situations but otherwise seem fairly neurotypical. Autism is often called a hidden disability, because it is often not at all obvious until you get to know the person that they have autism.

I would go into greater depth here about diagnosis, speech and language therapy and choosing the right school for your child, but that's what the rest of the book is for!

Early signs of ASC

Although autism is a lifelong condition, it can take a while for it to become apparent that your child has ASC and to go for a diagnosis. Some children are diagnosed from a relatively early age (before school age), while others are diagnosed as late as adolescence or adulthood. Possible signs to look out for include:

- Delayed speech
- Difficulty with social interactions
- Not making eye contact
- Not responding to their name or familiar voices
- Obsessive behaviour and attachments to specific toys/objects
- Challenging behaviours
- Sensory differences
- A need for routine

This, however, is not an exhaustive list, nor does it mean that if your child has the signs described that they have autism. If you're in any doubt, check out the section on diagnosis, and consider speaking to your doctor.

is for

'Bad' parenting (not)

Having a child with ASC doesn't make you any more or less likely to be a bad parent (equally, it doesn't make you any more or less likely to be a good parent). It does, however, vastly increase the chances that others will pass judgement on your parenting.

I'm sure many parents of children with ASC will recognise this scenario: you're out – let's say, in the queue for the till at the supermarket. Your child has had enough – the lights and the sounds and the sheer number of other people in the supermarket have created a perfect storm for sensory overload – and the tears have started. You can almost feel the daggers of other people's stares hitting your back. They're watching your child (and you). And they're judging your parenting skills.

> You won't be perfect, because no parent ever is. But if your child has ASC, the chances that they'll do or say something inappropriate in a social situation is greatly increased.

An old lady in the supermarket said that my son doesn't have autism; it's just my bad parenting style.

Sound familiar?

Let's face it, if you're a parent of a child with ASC and you haven't felt this, you're either very lucky, you're not paying attention, or you've developed a hide like a rhino.

The likelihood is, most of us will have been told at some point by someone (who is trying to be helpful) that the problem with our child is, plain and simple, bad parenting. Sometimes people will come straight out and say it. Sometimes it's just a look or a tut that leaves you in no doubt what they really think is the matter. Most often it's a total stranger, but not always. Sometimes it might be a parent or a grandparent. Sometimes it's even another of your children. Whoever says it and whatever they say, those words hurt. And sometimes, just for a moment, you've probably taken their words to heart and thought there's something in what they say. Maybe I *am* a bad parent. Maybe this is all my fault.

Before we go any further, let's clear one thing up. *You are not a bad parent just because your child has ASC.* You won't be perfect, because no parent ever is. But if your child has ASC, the chances that they'll do or say something inappropriate in a social situation is greatly increased. Much of the time, it's beyond your control. It isn't a parenting fail. It's a symptom of ASC.

But the sad fact is that this kind of judgement from strangers happens every single day and can have a damaging effect on families. I know of families who have become so paranoid that their child will have a meltdown if they go out and that they won't be able to deal with the looks and tuts and words of others, that they simply stop attempting to go out. It's much less hassle to stay inside and avoid others' prying eyes, they figure. And so they and their child miss out.

Stress

Having a child with ASC can provide extra challenges to parenting. For most parents, preparing for a day out is relatively simple – make sure everyone's been to the toilet, grab coats and maybe a packed lunch and then head out of the door. But often for parents of children with ASC, the process is much more involved. Choosing where to go will involve thinking through how your child will react to being in that place: will the shop be too noisy, the train too overcrowded, the museum too quiet?

You will often need time to prepare your child for the trip, explaining what will happen, how they might feel and what to do if they start to feel anxious. And then the morning of the outing will arrive and it's all too much and everything is so overwhelming that there's a meltdown before you even leave the house.

This is just one example, but there are hundreds of tiny battles that a parent of a child with ASC may face every single day. Getting dressed. Eating without being picky. Coaxing your child to go to school. Transitions. Everything involves you thinking a step or three ahead. Everything involves being braced for a meltdown. Everything involves you trying to remain calm while you're being shouted at, or kicked, or watching your child become upset. You are basically a mortal doing the work of a saint. And for us mere mortals, that kind of work can take a toll on our own ability to cope. We feel stressed. We find that we develop a shorter fuse. We feel bad about ourselves and our family. Sometimes we need help and understanding.

What to do

Ignore the ignorant

First of all, don't be put off by stares, tuts and comments. Easier said than done, I know. But this is important – for your child, for you, for your family, and for all the other families living with

> Let the comments wash over you; show that the world is a diverse place and that's okay.

children with ASC and a whole host of other conditions. If you allow the ignorance of others to stop you going out as a family, or to stop you doing certain activities, the people losing out are you and your family. Whereas if you go ahead and try to let the comments wash over you, you'll be showing everyone that the world is a diverse place and that's okay.

Be prepared

There are a whole host of strategies and resources which you can use to help make trips out a lot more bearable. I would really recommend looking at the National Autistic Society website, which has a really good section on family life. They give advice on all sorts of everyday activities such as going to the hairdressers and shopping. In most cases, more difficult behaviour is likely to be a result of anxiety. The anxiety might come from a number of places, but by understanding it and preparing your child for it, you might find that your trip out will be more pleasurable.

Get support

You are not alone (even if it might often feel that way). There will be hundreds of others who are going through the same thing as you, or who have been through it and have lived to tell the tale. There are hundreds of support groups around the country. Joining one could help you to feel like you're not battling alone. It might also help to share tips, strategies and successes with other parents.

Take care of yourself

It may sound patronising, but you have to think about yourself and your own wellbeing. You will be a much better parent, much more able to react calmly and logically to your child's needs, if you are not at the end of your tether. In reality, most people tend to prioritise pretty much everything else above their own mental health. Take some time to yourself, wherever you can. If you feel like you're struggling to cope, say something. It isn't a weakness to admit that you need help.

Autism-friendly events

There are all sorts of places up and down the country which run autism-friendly performances and events. A quick internet search should find you autism-friendly events at theatres, cinemas, soft play centres, sports grounds, music venues, museums and a whole lot more. You can also find autism-friendly holidays.

Bullying

The shocking truth is that, for various reasons, children with ASC are twice as likely to be bullied as those without ASC. However, by being aware of the warning signs and what you can do to help, you can make a big difference.

What is bullying?

The Anti-Bullying Alliance defines bullying as 'the repetitive, intentional hurting of one person or group by another person or group, where the relationship involves imbalance of power. Bullying can be physical, verbal or physiological. It can happen face-to-face or through cyberspace.'

Why are children with ASC more at risk?

Unfortunately, there are a number of factors which put children with ASC at greater risk of being bullied. Firstly, children with ASC often have challenges with communication, which can make it difficult both to negotiate difficult situations and to understand the motivations and intentions of someone else. They can also find it difficult to read non-verbal cues such as facial expression and tone of voice, meaning they're not always clear when someone is making fun of them. In addition, despite ASC being termed an invisible disability, as children with ASC grow older, it often starts to become obvious to their peers that they are different. Children with ASC may sometimes do things which other children think are odd, such as stimming (see page 148) or saying inappropriate things. These types of differences are something that bullies often tend to pick up on and use as their ammunition. Also, as children with ASC often like to play alone, this can make them easy prey for a bully, as they often don't have a group of friends around who might step in to stop the bullying.

> Children with ASC are twice as likely to be bullied as those without ASC.

How can I spot if my child is being bullied?

It can be difficult to spot whether your child is being bullied. Your child may not realise that they are being bullied, having misread the intentions of the bully. Sometimes it can be difficult for your child to tell you they are being bullied because they find it difficult to communicate. Therefore, you may need to keep an eye out for tell-tale signs that your child is being bullied. These are some of the signs you might see:

- Reluctance to go to school – the child may make excuses or suffer from physical symptoms of anxiety such as stomach aches
- The child might become more anxious – they may show an increase in obsessional and repetitive behaviour

- Lost or spoiled/dirty clothing and possessions
- The child seems stressed or depressed
- Quality of schoolwork may suffer

What should I do if I suspect my child is being bullied?

Your first step should be to speak to your child. Hopefully this way you can establish what happened, who was involved and (if it is happening at school) what the staff have done about it. Making notes on what your child has said is a good idea and may help when you raise the issue with school staff. It may be that during the conversation with your child you discover they are being bullied but aren't aware of this, in which case you should explain to them what bullying is. It is also a good idea to agree a way forward with your child, so that the problem can be addressed. Both social stories and comic strip conversations may be of use in this.

Your next port of call should be your child's school to make them aware of what has happened. Try to remain calm and lay out the facts as your child told you (referring to the notes you made previously will be helpful). During this meeting you should be able to agree a way forward and school staff may be able to help you with suggestions of things you can do to help your child.

Can children with ASC be bullies too?

Children with ASC can be bullies, just like other children. Often this might come out of not understanding the social rules of the playground. For example, they might try to make other children play with them when they don't want to. It can also come out of frustration that other children don't play their games the way the child with ASC wants the game played, and the child with ASC becomes aggressive.

is for

Cause

Hear that metallic ripping noise? Don't worry about it. That's just the sound of me opening an enormous can of worms. Because this is perhaps one of the most contentious areas regarding autism.

But before we move onto the controversial ground, let me just say that there is currently no known cause for autism. None. It could be genetic. It could be environmental. Or it could be something else entirely. Clear? No, thought not.

The controversy centres around some theories which you don't have to search far on the internet to find.

The most widespread theory is that autism is caused by vaccination. A lot of people still believe that the measles, mumps and rubella (MMR) vaccine is the cause. The theory was first postulated back in 1998 by Andrew Wakefield, a gastroenterologist, who was subsequently struck off the UK Medical Register. The link was never proven, however, and there are a number of issues which can be taken with his study and the conclusions it draws. Most of all, the correlation between autism and having had the MMR vaccine seems to be coincidental. The age at which children are given the vaccine is the same age at which most children begin to show symptoms of ASC. The two are not necessarily linked.

The surge in diagnosis of children with ASC in the time since the MMR vaccine was introduced (1987) is more easily explained by greater public awareness of ASC and the change in methods of diagnosis.

One thing is for certain though: by putting this theory out there, Wakefield caused a stir. The autism/MMR vaccine link was broadcast around the world on television and radio and in newspapers and magazines. Parents, understandably, sat up and took notice. Despite the fact that the scientific evidence appears to stack up against Wakefield's conclusions, his suggested link seems to have become embedded in the public consciousness. Even a quick look at the internet will show that this theory is still going strong. Whether or not you think there is a link, a quick cost–benefit analysis of the MMR vaccination versus autism indicates that no-one has died from autism, but plenty have died from not having had the vaccine.

There are other more likely causes of autism – genetic factors, for instance. Most researchers believe that your genetic make-up can make you more likely to develop ASC. Indeed, ASC has been known to run in families. Siblings of children with ASC often develop ASC too. But there isn't one single gene that causes autism. In fact, scientists currently estimate that there are between 200 and 400 different genes which could cause autism.

Some researchers believe that where a genetic disposition to ASC exists, exposure to specific environmental triggers can cause ASC to develop. Possible triggers include medication taken during pregnancy (such as sodium valproate, a drug used to treat epilepsy among other things) or premature birth. However, there is no conclusive evidence to link maternal infections or pollution (e.g. drugs taken during pregnancy) to an increased risk of developing ASC.

Which, as I said before, leaves the whole causation question as clear as mud. We genuinely don't know what causes ASC. And even if we did, would it change anything for our children?

> There is currently no known cause for autism.

Co-existing conditions

People with ASC may also be diagnosed with other conditions, which co-exist alongside ASC. Some of the most common are listed below. If you think your child may have a co-existing condition as well as ASC, speak to your GP or Special Educational Needs Coordinator (SENCo) and they may be able to help you seek a referral and put in place useful strategies for your child.

Attention deficit hyperactivity disorder (ADHD)

ADHD is quite common in children with ASC. Children with ADHD usually have difficulty with either inattentiveness or hyperactivity/impulsivity, although they can have difficulties in both areas. ADHD can make home and school life difficult.

What to look for

- Finding it difficult to follow instructions
- Making careless mistakes
- Difficulty concentrating on and finishing tasks
- Being easily distracted/distracting others
- Lack of organisation (e.g. losing things, forgetting things)
- Being fidgety
- Being overactive or always on the go
- Talking excessively
- Interrupting others when talking
- Calling out answers
- Difficulty waiting for their turn or waiting in line

What can I do?

If your child is given a diagnosis of ADHD, the doctor may discuss medication with you. They will also recommend strategies that may help your child at home and at school. These may include considering where the child is seated in the classroom (are they away from distractions?), allowing movement breaks, breaking tasks down into manageable chunks, making sure important information is written down, agreeing a behaviour plan, building self-esteem, and allowing a fidget toy in lessons.

Down syndrome

The chances are that you will find out about a diagnosis of Down syndrome long before you are given a diagnosis of ASC, as most diagnoses are made soon after birth. Screening tests during pregnancy may already have made you aware of an increased chance of having a baby with Down syndrome.

Down syndrome is a lifelong condition which causes developmental and learning delays. There is no cure, but children with Down syndrome can be supported to become more independent and live a happy life. The degree of learning difficulty varies from child to child, but childhood milestones, such as walking, talking and toileting, are usually delayed.

Epilepsy

Epilepsy is a condition where someone has seizures that start in the brain. It is estimated that somewhere between 20 and 40% of those with ASC also have epilepsy (a wide range, I know). This compares to around 1% of the population overall. Some behavioural traits of ASC, such as flapping and staring straight ahead, can be mistaken for seizures. If you are concerned that your child may have epilepsy, make sure you see a specialist.

Dyslexia

Dyslexia is a difference in the way information is processed, stored and accessed by the brain, which affects the learning of literacy and language skills. Signs to look out for include reading and writing slowly, confusing the order of letters and words, reversing letters (e.g. writing *d* as *b*), and having difficulty spelling, getting thoughts down on paper, following sequences of instructions, and with organisation. Dyslexia is a lifelong condition, but with support, those with it can learn to make adaptations to help.

Dyspraxia

Dyspraxia is a condition which affects movement and coordination and can affect speech. It can make life more difficult as balance, movement, self-help skills (such as dressing) and tasks such as writing, drawing, typing and grasping small objects can be affected. It is also common to have difficulties with some organisational skills, time management, and dealing with emotions and social situations. Treatment may include occupational therapy and speech and language therapy, and emotional support may help.

Learning disabilities

People with ASC may have different levels of learning disabilities, or none at all. Learning disabilities can affect different aspects of life, including social understanding, life skills and academic success. For many people with ASC, some support will be necessary, but they will be able to live a mostly independent life. Others may require long-term specialist support.

Fetal anti-convulsant syndrome (FACS)

FACS is caused by the mother taking anti-convulsants (anti-seizure drugs) during pregnancy, though not all children exposed to these drugs in pregnancy will be affected. Symptoms include delayed speech and language, and difficulties with social interaction, memory and attention.

Fragile X syndrome

People with Fragile X syndrome may have mild to severe learning disabilities. Many of the behaviours of those with Fragile X syndrome are the same as commonly seen in ASC: difficulties with social situations, avoidance of eye contact, impulsiveness, preference for routine, repetitive and restrictive activities and hand flapping. The drivers behind these behaviours are different, however. For instance, the cause of difficulties with social situations for someone with Fragile X syndrome is social anxiety, as opposed to a lack of social understanding. Fragile X syndrome is a different diagnosis with a known genetic cause and a blood test can determine whether your child has Fragile X.

Sensory processing disorder (SPD)

This is a neurological disorder that results from the brain being unable to integrate information received from the sensory systems. Characteristics of SPD differ between people, but they are either hyposensitive (under-sensitive) or hypersensitive (over-sensitive) to sensory input. SPD can affect one sense or any combination of them. It can range in severity from causing difficulties with daily functioning to being barely noticeable as a difficulty.

Cognitive behavioural therapy (CBT)

CBT is a talking therapy. The idea is that by talking through problems that may seem overwhelming to an individual, they can learn to adapt and manage them better. It's usually used to combat anxiety and depression and as people with ASC can struggle with both of these conditions, CBT is often helpful.

How does it work?

Essentially CBT works on the problems someone is currently facing which may seem overwhelming. By talking through their problems with them, the therapist aims to help them become more positive in the way they view and deal with them.

CBT sessions are usually weekly or fortnightly and may last for half an hour to an hour each. The therapist helps the patient to break their problem down into smaller parts (physical feelings, thoughts and actions), analysing how they respond to them and whether this is helpful to the patient or not. The therapist will then work with the patient on how to change unhelpful behaviours, feelings and thoughts. The onus is then on the patient to go and put this into practice, reporting back in the next session. Ultimately, the aim of this therapy is that the patient is taught to apply the analytical skills to help themselves in the future.

How is it used with people with ASC?

CBT can work well with people with ASC because it focuses in on specific problems and how the patient is currently dealing with them, then offers practical advice on how to tackle them differently. In some ways, this follows a similar model to social stories, which also work well for people with ASC. CBT can help to explicitly teach social rules which someone with ASC may not have grasped.

It is common for people with ASC to get into restrictive and negative ways of thinking about themselves (e.g. 'If I don't try to interact with other people, I won't get it wrong', 'I am different from other people'). CBT can help to stop the patient from thinking in this way and to instead think in a more helpful and positive way.

CBT can also help with other ASC-related issues such as repetitive/ obsessive interests, self-care and difficult behaviour.

In order for CBT to be successful, the patient needs to be able to identify their emotions; have some insight into their own thoughts, feelings and behaviour; and to be motivated to try new approaches to problems. While autism can make it more challenging to undertake CBT, the skills that CBT teaches are really valuable to people with ASC.

Therapists can tailor the way they use CBT to suit the patient, so if they are working with a child with a diagnosis of ASC who is a very concrete thinker, the therapist can modify the therapy to be more concrete.

Comic strip conversations

Comic strip conversations are a tool for helping children with ASC to understand social situations which they are finding tricky. They were the brainchild of Carol Gray, who also came up with the idea of social stories (see page 136). They can help you and your child to do some detective work to find out what went wrong in a situation and to put in steps to make sure it doesn't go wrong in future.

When would I do one?

In my experience, a comic strip conversation is a useful tool to help unpick any social situation that has caused upset or difficulty. These can often be broken down into two types of scenario:

1   A social situation which the child doesn't understand and that you wish to help them with and teach them a more appropriate way of responding in future.

2   A situation which you can't currently get to the bottom of. (For instance, there may have been a fight and you don't know how or

why it began, and asking straight questions is not getting you straight answers.)

How do I do a comic strip conversation?

1 Start by drawing the people who were involved in the situation and where they were when it happened. Stick men and women are the name of the game here. It might be worth asking if there were other people around who saw what happened too.

2 After that, move onto what actually happened. Try to be as clear as possible in your questioning. It's usually best to draw the flash point of the situation to start with and work from there.

3 The next stage is to draw speech bubbles to show what was said by everyone involved, starting with the person who is the focus of the story. If you like, you can colour-code them to show the emotions which are associated with the words (see below for details).

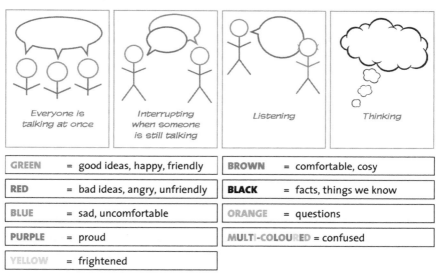

Everyone is talking at once	Interrupting when someone is still talking	Listening	Thinking

GREEN	= good ideas, happy, friendly	BROWN	= comfortable, cosy
RED	= bad ideas, angry, unfriendly	BLACK	= facts, things we know
BLUE	= sad, uncomfortable	ORANGE	= questions
PURPLE	= proud	MULTI-COLOURED	= confused
YELLOW	= frightened		

4 By now, you'll be starting to get an idea of what really happened (hopefully), so the next stage is to focus on what those involved were thinking. This may be tricky as people with ASC often find reading the thoughts and intentions of others difficult, so you may need to do some gentle guiding. If this still fails, you may need to say outright what those involved were likely to have been thinking. Draw thought bubbles to show what they were thinking. You may

wish to colour-code these to show the emotions that these thoughts demonstrate.

It is often at this point that the misunderstanding becomes clear – you'll see what the child's understanding of the situation was and be able to help them. It might also be the case that this is the point where you realise you need to know what happened before the incident. If so, you'll need to do the next step:

5 Your detective work may mean you need to draw earlier cells which show what led up to the incident. Do this in exactly the same way as before.

Hopefully once this is all done, you'll have identified exactly what the trigger was for the behaviour and you'll be able to help your child be prepared with a more appropriate way to react in future. One way to do this is to draw an alternative ending once the misunderstanding has been identified. This cell would focus on what would be an appropriate response if the situation arose in the future. You can also write a social story linked to the situation.

At every single stage, it is important that you ask questions to clarify exactly what happened. My tip would be to keep the questions as simple and plain as possible and try to stick to the facts.

Do I need to be able to draw?

Certainly not. It doesn't matter if you can't draw for toffee. As long as you can produce a stick man or woman, you will be fine. It might be an idea to have coloured pencils to hand, but other than that, all you need is patience.

Where can I find more information about comic strip conversations?

As with most things, a quick internet search will equip you with a wealth of resources and ideas. Carol Gray's book, *Comic Strip Conversations: Illustrated interactions that teach conversation skills to students with autism and related disorders*, is a good starting place. You'll also find information on comic strip conversations in my book, *Otis the Robot: The Manual*.

Cure

> *If there were a cure for Asperger's, I don't know if I'd want it. Humanity has prospered because of people with autistic traits. Without them, we wouldn't have put man on the moon or be running software programs. If we wiped out all the autistic people on the planet, I don't know how much longer the human race would last.*
>
> Chris Packham

It was tempting to just leave this section empty. Because, just to be clear, there isn't a cure for autism. There's no cure and no magic wand and no medicine which will make the autism go away. Autism is a lifelong condition. If you have autism now, you'll have it when you're older too. And for most people that's just fine, thank you very much. Most people with autism don't want a cure. Autism is one of the things that makes them the person they are. Take away the autism and you take away a part of their personality.

That's not to say nothing can be done though. In fact, there are loads of ways to make life easier for those with ASC. I would write about each of them here, but that's what the rest of the book is about!

D is for

Diagnosis

You've done the online quiz and it told you your child definitely has ASC. Your friend (whose nephew has a friend with ASC) says so too. Even the security guard at the local supermarket tells you your kid has ASC. They can't all be wrong, can they?

Well, yes they can, actually. They could also be right. In order to know for sure and to get a diagnosis of ASC, you'll need to see a few medical professionals. This chapter will look at the rollercoaster ride of diagnosis. Strap yourself in; it could be a bumpy ride.

Why go for a diagnosis?

To some, diagnosis is just a label, possibly even a stigma. To others, receiving a diagnosis is like putting the final piece in a jigsaw puzzle – finally everything makes sense. In all honesty, you couldn't say that either of those perspectives is wholly right or wholly wrong. Because, yeah, sure enough, autism *is* just a label. Once given the label, the child (or adult) with the diagnosis won't magically change overnight. There is no magic wand which the diagnosis unlocks which will help to cure autism. But, in most cases, the diagnosis will help you to understand your child a little better, and get more support for them.

And getting the right understanding and support for your child is vital. Having a diagnosis can make it much easier to get extra funding to support your child in school (see page 50 for information about EHCPs) and make sure that the school arrange the best provision for your child. Having a diagnosis can also be key in making sure you're able to get your child into the right kind of educational provision, whether that's a mainstream school, a mainstream school with a base, or a special school (see page 113 for more on finding the right school provision).

> To some, diagnosis is just a label, possibly even a stigma. To others, receiving a diagnosis is like putting the final piece in a jigsaw puzzle.

How to get a diagnosis

Getting referred

If your child is pre-school age and you think they may have autism, your first port of call will most likely be your health visitor, or failing that, your GP. They'll be able to talk through what you've observed and advise you on whether a referral is appropriate or not. For very young children, don't be surprised to be told to wait until your child is older before a diagnosis can be made. This is fairly common in my experience, because some of the behaviour traits which might mark out a child as having ASC can also be the character traits of a toddler. Therefore, if in any doubt, doctors would rather see if the symptoms persist over time: it is better to keep an open mind than make a misdiagnosis.

If your child is already at school, book an appointment to speak to your child's teacher or the school's Special Educational Needs Coordinator (SENCo). As at least one of them will have spent a significant amount of time looking after your child, they may have picked up on signs of autism too. They can then refer you onto the appropriate assessment service, which may depend on the age of your child.

Other people that you could try to approach would include speech and language therapists, educational psychologists, specialist language or behaviour teachers and occupational therapists. Each of these people will have enough experience and expertise in ASC to recognise the signs and will be able to signpost you in the right direction for referral.

Whoever you speak to, I'd recommend taking some time before you meet to note down what your concerns and observations are. This will be helpful to you (it'll stop you from drying up under pressure) and also to the professional you're meeting (more information will help them make a more informed judgement).

The assessment begins... kind of

So, you've secured a referral. You probably feel like a weight has been lifted from your shoulders. It feels like you're being listened to at last. You hadn't just imagined it; other people think the same as you. The wheels have been set in motion and surely the support you and your child need is just around the corner.

Well, sort of.

Before the assessment stage, there's another hoop to jump through. You will probably be sent some forms to fill in about your child, and may also be given some to hand over to the school to fill in. If your completed forms indicate that there are traits of autism, the case will go forward to assessment and you can expect to wait for an appointment. If not, the case will be closed.

So the forms have gone off. An assessment has been agreed. Now all you have to do is sit back and wait... possibly for a very long time.

Because, I'm afraid, at the time of writing, there are *long* waiting lists to be seen for assessment (although this may depend on your postcode and which way the wind is blowing). In some places, it is not unknown to wait for anything up to a year before the assessment takes place. The National Institute of Clinical Excellence (NICE) guidelines state the assessment should be within three months of referral, but that's not my experience, nor that of many others. One way to get around the waiting list – if you have the money – is to pay for a private assessment.

In the wait between referral and assessment, I'd recommend that you do some homework to get you prepared for the assessment meeting. If you have lots of reports on your child, dig them out and read through them again. If not, rack your brains, crack open the old photo albums, talk to other family members, school staff and friends and see what they remember. If you can make a note of these things, it will help you immensely in the assessment.

Now just sit back, relax and wait for your appointment. (What do you mean, you're not feeling relaxed?!)

The doctor will see you now

So either you waited a year, lucked out and got seen quickly, or paid to jump the queue. Congratulations – you made it. This is what to expect from the assessment.

The assessment will be carried out by a multi-disciplinary team of professionals who will be using the ICD-10 or DSM-V criteria, which are the main criteria for psychiatric assessment (worth an internet search). Already sounds intimidating, doesn't it? And sometimes it can feel that way too. If you think you might end up either clamming up or feeling intimidated by being faced by a team of professionals, I'd advise that you take someone with you to the meeting, to help even up the teams a little and provide some moral support.

Not all assessments will be alike. Some may happen across multiple meetings and others may be at just one appointment. Either way, the team of professionals will want to see your child. The nature of the assessment will differ depending on the age and ability of your child, but the team will want to do a physical examination, as well as interact with your child, focusing on social and communication skills and behaviours. If your child is young, this might involve playing with some jigsaws or a doll's house or toy cars. If your child is a teenager, it probably won't. While one member of the team interacts with your child, another will observe. At the end of the session, they'll score the behaviours and communication they've seen. As well as looking at traits of ASC, they'll be looking to rule out other possible diagnoses, which could include attachment disorders, anxiety disorders, hearing impairment and a host of other things.

The team will also want to speak to you, as the parent or guardian. They'll ask you tons of questions about the development and behaviour of your child, dating right back to birth. This is where the homework you did during the long wait to be seen will come in handy – having your crib sheet in front of you should mean you don't freeze when in the pressured situation of a meeting. Try to relax and tell them what you have noticed over the years that has led you to seek the assessment. The information you provide the team will also be scored.

You probably won't get an immediate diagnosis. The team will need to meet to discuss their findings. They'll have looked to rule out other conditions (physical, developmental and mental health) and will have scored the assessments. When you get feedback, you might be invited back to receive the report and the diagnosis in person, you might be contacted by phone or you might receive the report in the post. Finally, you'll have a diagnosis. Unless, of course, there is no diagnosis. Either way, don't underestimate the emotional impact this will have. Hearing what you've suspected all along can still be a devastating shock. A diagnosis can seem final. You might worry that you've got it all wrong. And if you don't get a diagnosis – well, that can feel just as bad. You'll feel like you're back at square one. You'll need support either way... which we'll come to in a minute.

But hang on a minute... you've got it wrong

Diagnosing autism isn't an exact science. Much of the assessment is based on the information provided to the assessment team, either by you, the educational setting or your child. Sometimes that evidence is an opinion, or a recollection (which could be crystal clear, murky or somewhere in between). This makes the assessment process a subjective one in many ways. This means the assessment isn't 100% accurate, 100% of the time. Sometimes you, as a parent, will know that the conclusion you've been given isn't right. So, if you're taken aback by the feedback you're given, if the picture you're given doesn't sound like the young person you know and love, say something. According to the NICE guidelines, the diagnosis team should seek a second opinion if there is some disagreement.

In reality, I've seen this in action on a few occasions. In one case, the diagnosis team thought that in a one-to-one situation, the child in question was able to show pretty much appropriate conversational skills and eye contact. The parental interview and school questionnaire suggested there were other concerns with social communication and adapting to change. No diagnosis was reached. In the feedback session, the school explained the difficulties the child would have in an actual social situation (rather than a clinical setting). The diagnosis team agreed to send someone into school to see what the child was like in a real social situation. When they walked into the classroom,

> The diagnosis team should seek a second opinion if there is some disagreement.

they found him hiding under a table, shoes off, humming to himself with his fingers in his ears. The team took this new evidence (and other new evidence too) into consideration and a diagnosis was reached.

Post-diagnosis blues

What happens once you have a diagnosis of ASC is another one of those postcode lotteries we hear about in the news. In some places you get little more than a report and a photocopied leaflet about autism. In others, you may get a follow-up appointment for you and your child, where the implications of the diagnosis are discussed. If you're lucky, you may also get signposted to some local support services. If you don't, I'd recommend a quick search on the internet to find local support groups, social media groups and so on. You'll find there are loads. If you choose to join any, you may just find they're a lifesaver. When you're in the middle of dealing with yet another meltdown, it can feel like a very lonely place to be. Support groups (whether in the real world or online) can help you to see that you're not alone, that thousands of others are experiencing similar things or have gone through them and come out the other side wiser. Sometimes, that's enough to provide you with the strength you need. Other times, someone will recommend something to you that you have never considered that ends up changing your life for the better.

Where on the spectrum does my child sit?

If a diagnosis is reached, it will most likely simply state autism spectrum disorder (ASD): a catch-all term for the many different presentations of autism. Not so long ago, you might have been given a diagnosis of high-functioning autism, Asperger syndrome, autistic disorder, pervasive developmental disorder not otherwise specified or childhood disintegrative disorder. Then there is pathological demand avoidance, which is not recognised as a separate condition, but is regarded by many to be a behaviour profile within the autism spectrum. The presentations of any two people on the autism spectrum can be hugely different. So can the strategies that work with any two people – don't be afraid to shop around for strategies that work for you and your child. Doing some research to find out exactly where on the spectrum your child is may help to find the most useful support and strategies. The easiest way to do this is to read up on different presentations of autism on the internet (the National Autistic Society website is a good starting point).

Should I tell my child?

This is the million-dollar question. Of course, in many cases, the decision is taken out of your hands by the fact that your child may be old enough to understand exactly what's going on and that they have been given a diagnosis. But many children are given a diagnosis before they are old enough or cognitively ready to understand what it means. For instance, they may have been diagnosed at the age of five, completely and blissfully unaware of what has just happened. As they get older, they may begin to realise that they are 'different' to the majority of their peers. It isn't uncommon for a child approaching adolescence to begin to question, for example, why they have a teaching assistant working with them when others don't. This is a common point where parents make the decision: do I tell my child of their diagnosis, and exactly how they're different? Or do I shield them from it?

There are valid arguments on both sides. Many see a diagnosis as little more than a label and wonder how it could be of use to a young person. They think that it will be a stigma rather than anything positive. Indeed, many young people with a diagnosis will themselves reject their diagnosis (see page 101). Others feel that knowing their own diagnosis is important. It can give the young person ownership of their condition, and that ownership can help them to adapt to the world around them.

Diet

There will be many people reading this sentence right now for whom mealtimes are a time of day they dread. For families with a child who has ASC, mealtimes can often be a battleground. Perhaps your child won't eat any food that is touching another type of food. Perhaps your child will only eat orange foods this week. Maybe your child will only eat pasta and mayonnaise. Or perhaps you've been told by your kid's school that sending in a lunchbox containing a packet of ham and a chocolate biscuit isn't good enough. Then again, perhaps you're lucky and your child eats anything and everything you put in front of them… whether it's food or not (which can be a problem all of its own).

Whatever the mealtime specifics in your household, one trait of ASC can be restricted and rigid eating patterns.

Why is my child a fussy eater?

Being a fussy eater is common in children, not just for those with ASC. While it can be frustrating, it is not always anything to be overly concerned about. As long as your child is eating food from each of the main food groups and they are healthy, fussy eating may not be a problem.

When should I be worried?

Mostly, it's just common sense. It would be wise to seek help if your child:

- is losing weight or not growing well
- is not eating from each of the main food groups
- is gaining weight excessively
- has tooth decay caused by their diet
- is constipated
- seems tired or anaemic
- struggles with the physical act of eating (e.g. chokes on food)
- is missing out on school or social situations due to issues with eating.

> As long as your child is eating food from each of the main food groups and they are healthy, fussy eating may not be a problem.

If you are concerned, speak to a GP, dietician or other medical professional.

What can I do to help my child get a balanced diet?

A good starting place would be to gain as deep an understanding of the problem as possible. One way to do this might be to keep a food diary. As well as recording what your child eats and when, it might be worth considering and including information about other environmental factors and sensory issues such as noise, environment, social factors, obsessions/routines (are there particular meals, places, foods, plates that are a problem?) and the way the food is presented.

Once you think you have identified the root cause of the eating problem, you could try using a social story to explain why it is important to eat a balanced diet. Having an idea of the root cause of the eating issue may also help you to identify small changes that you can make. For example, if you find that your child doesn't eat well at school because of the amount of noise in the lunch room, you can speak to the school and try to negotiate either an alternative time or place for them to eat.

It may also be worth explaining the different food groups and why we need them to your child. There are plenty of visual representations of the food groups which could be useful in helping you and your child make choices about what to eat. While it is easy to slip into describing foods as *good* or *bad*, *healthy* or *unhealthy*, this can prove to be a hindrance with children with ASC as they may take it too literally.

Some parents have success using reward systems. A simple visual reward system (such as a sticker chart) can prove a motivating way to encourage children to try foods from different food groups.

Of vital importance for all children is that the adult models eating a wide range of foods. If your child sees you eating a balanced diet, they will get the message that eating a balanced diet is best. If, however, they see you avoiding certain foods, they will get the message that this is acceptable behaviour. You could also extend this to cooking and preparing foods. If you can get your child interested in cooking a wide range of foods, you stand a much better chance of them having a healthy relationship with food.

If the issue is to do with overeating, you could try a number of things – such as limiting food portions and keeping food out of reach, so snacking between meals is controlled by you. It may also be worth setting a food timetable, which sets out the times for meals and snacks.

If undereating is the issue, you could try increasing portion sizes and using larger plates, to make the portion seem smaller. In this case, it may also be useful to help your child to get more involved in the preparation of food.

Could my child have an eating disorder?

There is research that suggests there is an overlap between eating disorders and autism (see page 47 for more on this topic). If you're worried about your child, speak to your GP or another healthcare professional.

My child is literally eating me out of house and home – starting with the walls...

Some children with ASC may also have pica. This is when they eat or mouth items which are inedible. The range of what they might mouth or eat is almost never-ending, and includes some extremely unpalatable things.

There can be a number of reasons behind pica, which can include stress and anxiety, iron deficiency, relieving pain, attention seeking, demand avoidance, seeking sensory input and not growing out of (or late development of) infant mouthing behaviours.

What can I do to help if my child has pica?

A simple and firm 'no', without making eye contact, may help to stop your child eating or mouthing something inappropriate. Sometimes diversion or distraction can also help stop a child when they are mouthing or eating things you don't want them to. It may help to offer safer items for your child to mouth; carrot sticks or chew toys might be suitable options.

If you notice that the behaviour occurs when demands are put on your child, try reducing the demands. Alternatively, it may be that adding more structure to the day may help your child.

The reason behind pica may be physical and so it is worth visiting a dentist to rule out pain or discomfort which could be causing your child to mouth things. Similarly, your GP will be able to help rule out any nutritional deficiencies and will be able to refer you to an occupational therapist, who can help with strategies to cope with pica.

is for

Eating disorders

There is growing understanding that there is an overlap between the symptoms of eating disorders and the traits of autism. That isn't to say that those with ASC will develop an eating disorder, or vice versa. As yet, no direct link has been drawn between the two conditions. However, this is an area where research is still taking place, which will hopefully inform our understanding of how the two conditions can co-exist. At present, estimates of how many people with an eating disorder have ASC vary wildly, from 2% up to 20%. However, some believe that many girls with eating disorders may have missed out on a diagnosis of ASC when they were younger and so the figure could be higher.

What is an eating disorder?

According to the NHS, an eating disorder is an abnormal attitude towards food which leads someone to change their behaviour towards food and eating habits, which is detrimental to their health. The most common eating disorders are anorexia, bulimia and binge eating disorder. While the common perception is that eating disorders are caused by images of stick-thin models in the media, the reality is much more complex. Societal pressures to be thin may be one factor, environmental factors may be another. It is possible that ASC, or traits associated with ASC, may be another exacerbating factor for some people.

So what's the link to ASC?

Research shows that people with ASC and those with an eating disorder often both have difficulties understanding and interpreting social cues. In a recent study in Sweden, MRI scans showed similarities between people with ASC and people with anorexia in the part of the brain linked to social cognition, which is how we think about, store and process information about other people and social situations. The similarities shown by the MRI scans indicate that both groups have some difficulties in the way they deal with social situations. Both groups also tend to fixate on tiny details, making it hard for them to see the big picture. As well as this, people with ASC and those with an eating disorder often crave rules, routines and rituals and have a very rigid way of thinking. Both groups tend to have increased anxiety.

While ASC traits might not be the root cause of an eating disorder, scientists think they may worsen other factors which can lead to and maintain eating disorders. For instance, factors such as rigid thinking, obsessiveness, a need for routine, repetitive interests and anxiety – which are common in people with ASC – can contribute to maintaining an eating disorder.

Studies have shown that patients with anorexia who have recovered and are now at a healthy weight still show the traits mentioned above after recovery. What isn't so clear at the moment, however, is whether these traits were present before they developed an eating disorder.

Treatment of eating disorders for those with ASC traits

It is thought that having ASC (or traits of the condition) may make treatment and recovery from an eating disorder more difficult. This could be partly because many of the interventions currently used to treat eating disorders are social in nature, but also possibly because the traits of rigid thinking and repetitive behaviour can make it difficult to make changes to behaviour.

It's hoped that a greater understanding of the link between eating disorders and ASC will help to inform new approaches to treating eating disorders, which are designed specifically with ASC in mind. This may lead to experts in ASC and eating disorders working together in the treatment of patients.

Gender balance

One interesting difference between those who have ASC and eating disorders is the gender balance. Boys are far more likely to be diagnosed with ASC than girls. However, girls are far more likely to have an eating disorder than boys: 1 in 250 girls will develop an eating disorder, compared to 1 in 2000 boys. This leads to the question: could some girls with an eating disorder also have undiagnosed ASC? There is some suggestion that some girls with traits of ASC are being misdiagnosed or overlooked as they present with symptoms of anorexia. Certainly there are cases where girls develop an eating disorder and their ASC is only diagnosed as a consequence. This will be an area which current research will help to shed some light on.

How do I know whether my child has an eating disorder?

Here are some key things to look out for in your child:

- Being secretive about food (e.g. saying that they've already eaten or will eat later to avoid eating at home)
- Being obsessive about food
- Having a distorted body image (e.g. thinking that they're fat when they aren't)
- Missing meals
- Going to the toilet immediately after meals
- Being tired or struggling to concentrate
- Weighing themselves repeatedly and looking at themselves in the mirror
- Looking at pro-anorexia websites
- Being defensive about their eating or weight
- Eating only low-calorie foods
- Feeling uncomfortable about eating in public places
- Becoming very withdrawn
- Starting to exercise excessively

What can I do if I'm concerned my child has an eating disorder?

Eating disorders can potentially be life-threatening, so seeking the right support and services is vital. Usually, someone with an eating disorder will require the intervention of a number of professionals – which could include dieticians, psychologists, psychotherapists and nurses to name a few. The first step is to speak to your GP, who will be able to refer you to the right service and help you access support.

You'll also find a wealth of information and guidance on the internet around eating disorders. The charity Beat also provides helplines, support groups and message boards.

Education, Health and Care Plan (EHCP)

An EHCP is a legal document which entitles children and young people (up to the age of 25) with SEND to extra support and (usually) extra funding. As you might imagine, this can be a very good thing. It is fairly common for children who have a diagnosis of ASC to have an EHCP. However, not all children with ASC will need one.

Getting an EHCP isn't just as easy as asking for it, though, and this chapter will try to explain how to get one and what to do with it.

How do I know if my child needs an EHCP?

In short, an application for an education, health and care (EHC) assessment is usually made in cases where a child struggles to cope with the day-to-day demands of school because of a special educational need or disability, and significant extra support is required.

> An EHCP entitles children and young people with SEND to extra support and (usually) extra funding.

Who can apply for an EHCP?

Most frequently, the decision to go for an EHC assessment will be made by the school, with the support of parents. It is possible, although much less common, for parents to make the application directly themselves. If a child is over the age of 16, they themselves may request that the process of application be started.

How will the process start?

I would venture that this process should start with a meeting between the school and the parents, where an agreement is reached that despite the support a child is already getting, they're not making adequate progress. This meeting should usually be with the Special Educational Needs Coordinator (SENCo), who will fill you in on how the process works. At this point, you may plan together to make sure that you have all the evidence that will be required. Your child might already have been seen by educational psychologists, speech and language therapists, Child and Adolescent Mental Health Services (CAMHS) and many others. If this is the case, the school may simply need to collate the evidence and present it to the local authority (LA) for consideration. If the school doesn't yet have enough evidence to go for an EHCP, they may at this stage plan to invite professionals to assess and work with your child. When the school has all the information they think they need, they will send it to the LA, where it will go to a panel (see below).

Timescales

As soon as the LA receive the application, the clock starts ticking. They have 20 weeks from the moment they receive the application to get the finished EHCP issued, should they agree to one.

There are other statutory timescales which they should adhere to, too. The diagram below should help to explain what the LA should do and when.

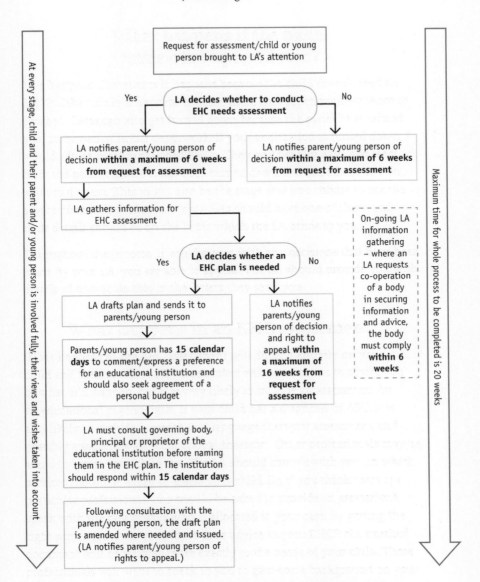

Statutory timescales for EHC needs assessment and EHC plan development (SEND Code of Practice, 2017)

What evidence is needed?

The school (or whoever is requesting the assessment) should provide evidence that the appropriate services have been involved with the child. For a child with a diagnosis of ASC, this could include an educational psychologist, speech and language therapist, paediatrician and CAMHS.

It might also include specialist autism services, occupational therapy and any other services relevant.

As well as these reports, the school should provide evidence that they have implemented the advice provided by the professionals whose reports they have received, and that they have evaluated these strategies and interventions.

They will also be expected to include the costings of the support they provide for your child. This should show that your child's school is putting in place support above and beyond what could be expected at the lower level of SEN support.

The school will also provide the key worker form (the name and format may vary in different LAs), which they will fill in with your help. This form sets out the background, strengths, needs, outcomes and aspirations of your child, and if the application is successful it will help to shape what the finished EHCP looks like.

Information about attendance is also submitted along with any relevant information about social services involvement and records of challenging behaviours.

Who is on the panel?

The panel is a multi-disciplinary group of professionals who read each SEND case and make a decision on what should happen. They don't get to meet the children but will be provided with all the evidence to read. In the first instance, the panel will simply be asked to make a decision on whether the child's case merits going forward to an EHC assessment. They will be looking to see that the appropriate professionals have been involved and that their advice has been sought and implemented by the school. They'll also be looking to make sure that the level of need is beyond that which can be met at school support level on the school's SEN register. You will not be invited to the panel, but a SEN caseworker should advise you of the outcome.

The LA has six weeks from receiving the application to make a decision on whether to assess or not.

What happens if the panel turns our request down?

This happens. Sometimes it happens because the child doesn't need an EHCP. Other times it happens because there isn't yet enough evidence to proceed. Cases can also get turned down because the panel have missed vital information in the paperwork. If your application is turned down, I would advise speaking to the SENCo. They will usually have had feedback from the panel on why it has been turned down and can advise you on what to do next. This might also be the stage that you choose to ask the advice of an independent adviser – LAs should have one of these, and their details should be on the letter which the LA sends to you.

Throughout the process, if you disagree with any decisions that have been made by your LA, you are able to appeal. The LA should provide you with details of how to do this in the letters they send you.

What happens in an EHC assessment?

What happens in the EHC assessment will depend entirely on your child and their needs. A SEN caseworker will contact you to advise you of what will happen, but it is very likely to include an assessment by an educational psychologist. If your child has a diagnosis of ASC, it is also likely to include a speech and language therapist assessment, and possibly another by an occupational therapist. Other professionals may be asked to assess your child too. The LA should consult with you on which services should be asked to assess your child. So, if you think there is a particular professional who should be asked to provide an assessment, speak with the caseworker who is allocated to your case. By getting the right professionals to contribute their advice to your EHCP, the finished document will be tailored more exactly to the needs of your child. These professionals will want to speak to you to gain some background on your child, their strengths, needs and aspirations. The assessments will focus on what the strengths and needs of your child are, what their long-term outcomes should be and what support would be most appropriate to help them meet these outcomes. You will also be asked to provide evidence to support this and so will the school.

The LA has a further six weeks to carry out the assessment.

Then what?

Next comes the planning stage. From the reports received (including your input via the key worker form or similar), the EHCP coordinator drafts an EHCP. They will send it to you and you will have 15 days to respond with any suggested changes, and a choice of school for your child. The LA should also be available to meet you to discuss the plan.

After this, the case will go back to the panel – the decision-making group. As before, the panel will be made up of a multi-disciplinary group of professionals and you won't be invited to attend. This time, they'll be looking to see whether they believe that an EHCP should be issued and what level of funding should be attached to the EHCP. This is the funding the school will receive to top up the funding which they're already putting in to support your child. Different LAs have different methods for allocating funds to EHCPs, but often they will give a band which equates to both a monetary figure (which the school will receive) and a notional number of teaching assistant (TA) hours which this is equivalent to. The school you have asked to be named in the EHCP will be consulted to see whether they can meet the child's needs and will have 15 days to reply. If they decide they can't, you can appeal against the decision.

After any last-minute changes have been made, the LA will issue the final EHCP. They have 20 weeks from first receiving the application to issue the final EHCP. If they decide not to issue the plan, the whole process should have happened within 16 weeks from the LA receiving the initial request. If this is the case, the outcomes in the plan should be used by the school to structure support.

How many hours of support should my child get?

The EHCP will probably have a notional number of TA hours on it. The amount of support your child receives should be close to this number. The number of hours which has been allocated by the LA is notional for a couple of reasons. Firstly, not all TAs earn the same hourly rate, so the amount of hours the funding covers differs from one to another. Secondly, although many children with an EHCP will benefit from one-to-one support, and some may not be able to function in school without it, this is not the only way the funding can be used. In fact, for many children, the funding is best used in a number of ways – perhaps some one-to-one support, some small-group work and some specialist equipment. If you think your child is being short-changed in terms of support, make sure you speak to the school.

Annual reviews

Each year, the EHCP will be reviewed in a meeting. This is called an annual review (see page 6).

is for

Facts (and myths)

Most people with ASC prefer to deal with facts; things that can be proven, information which follows logic and doesn't allow much room for misunderstanding. Researching this book, I've come across plenty of facts about ASC, plus many grey areas which are still up for interpretation, debate and argument, and also a fair few myths. Let's start with some of the facts, which were correct at time of writing in the UK:

- Autism literally means 'selfism'.
- Autism was first used as a term in 1911 by Eugen Bleuler, a Swiss psychiatrist.
- There are more than 700,000 people in the UK with ASC. That's more than one in 100, or 1.1%.
- Autism is a spectrum disorder, meaning that there are a wide range of presentations. No two people with a diagnosis of autism are the same; autism varies from person to person.
- At present, between four and five times more males are diagnosed with autism than females.
- 70% of children with autism are educated in mainstream schools. The rest are either in specialist provision or not in education.
- More than 11% of children with SEN in state schools have an ASC diagnosis.
- Around 90% of people with autism also have sensory issues.

- The cause of autism is not known.
- There is no cure for autism.
- You can't tell if someone has autism just by looking at them – therefore, many people call it a hidden disability.
- 17% of children with autism have been excluded from school.
- 16% of adults with autism are in paid full-time employment.
- Around 50% of those with autism also suffer from depression, anxiety or other mental health problems.
- 60% of teachers do not feel that they have had adequate training to effectively teach children with autism.
- 35% of teachers think it is becoming more difficult to access specialist support for children with autism.
- Primary school children with autism are twice as likely as those without autism to be bullied at school.
- Less than one in four school leavers with autism go into further or higher education.
- Autism is the fastest growing developmental disorder – greater numbers of people are being diagnosed than at any time in the past.

Myths

Whether you're surfing the internet, standing in the playground, chatting with friends and family or watching the television, you're bound to come across some of the many myths which surround autism. Some of these myths may be blatantly untrue, but others are harder to pin down. So, I've decided to take some of the more persistent myths and bust them with a few more well-aimed facts.

Myth	Fact
We are currently in the grip of an autism epidemic.	The prevalence of autism diagnosis has increased. This is most likely due to increased understanding and access to medical professionals who can diagnose ASC.
All people with autism are alike.	Autism is a spectrum disorder. There is an infinite variety of presentations. Therefore, no two people with a diagnosis of autism are the same.
Your child will grow out of autism.	Autism is a lifelong condition – if you have it as a child, you will have it as an adult.
Children with autism should be in a special school.	70% of children with autism are educated in mainstream schools. The rest are in specialist provision or not in education.
Autism is caused by vaccines, specifically MMR. Autism is caused by bad parenting.	The cause of autism is not currently known (see page 24).
Autism can be cured.	There is no cure for autism.
Autism only affects boys.	Girls can have autism, but currently between four and five times as many boys as girls are diagnosed with autism. Having said this, understanding and diagnosis of ASC in girls is increasing (see page 70).
Autism is a mental illness.	Autism is a neurodevelopmental disorder – this essentially means that the development of the brain or central nervous system is impaired.
People with autism don't have feelings or care about other people.	People with autism have the same feelings as other people, but sometimes they can have trouble reading their own and/or others' feelings.
People with autism are not as intelligent as those without. All children with Asperger syndrome are geniuses.	Autism affects people regardless of intelligence (also regardless of race, gender, sexuality, religion or social class).
People with autism can't form relationships.	People with autism can struggle with the many unwritten rules of relationships, but that doesn't mean they can't form them. They have husbands/wives/girlfriends/boyfriends/friends just like everyone else.
People with autism are anti-social.	People with autism find social situations more difficult than those without and sometimes social interactions can seem awkward. However, people with autism generally like the company of others.

Financial assistance

The good news is that there are many financial benefits which parents and carers of young people with ASC may be eligible for. The bad news is that the benefits system is prone to frequent and complicated change, and so the best thing to do is to look online at www.gov.uk to see which benefits you or your child may be eligible for. Here is a rundown of some:

Universal Credit

Universal Credit is being introduced at the time of writing. It replaces six other benefits and will be paid monthly. You may be eligible for Universal Credit as a parent or carer. If your child is over the age of 16 and has ASC, they may be eligible to claim it.

Employment and Support Allowance

This is for people over 16 (and under pension age) who cannot work or have a limited ability to work because of disability or for health reasons. This benefit replaces Incapacity Benefit. It can only be claimed if nobody is claiming tax credits or Child Benefit for you, so it is worth getting advice on whether or not this will leave you better or worse off before claiming.

Disability Living Allowance (DLA)

This is being abolished for adults but is still available for children (up to the age of 16). DLA can be claimed if your child has additional care needs or has difficulty walking because of disability or a health condition. Many – but not all – children with ASC qualify for DLA. This benefit is not means-tested.

Carer's Allowance

If your child is awarded DLA (middle or highest care rate), you may be able to claim Carer's Allowance, if you care for your child for more than 35 hours per week and you are not earning more than £116 net pay per week (correct at time of writing).

Personal Independence Payment

This is a non-means-tested benefit which has replaced the DLA for people over 16. It is available to working-age people (16–64) and can be claimed regardless of whether you are working or in full-time education. It is made up of two components – daily living and mobility – and you may be eligible for either or both. If you want to find out whether your child may be eligible, your first step is to call the Department for Work and Pensions. If you're unable to telephone, you can make the initial claim in writing (the National Autistic Society website has a template letter for this). After this, there is a form to fill in and a face-to-face assessment.

If you're in doubt about your eligibility to claim or how to claim any of the benefits, I'd recommend visiting www.gov.uk or www.citizensadvice.org.uk for details. Alternatively, the National Autistic Society website (www.autism.org.uk) has a lot of information about benefits on its website.

What if my son or daughter is unable to look after their own benefits?

If your son or daughter is 16 or over and receives benefits, but is unable to look after their own benefit claim, it is possible for another adult to apply to be their appointee. An appointee is someone who is appointed to look after all aspects of another person's benefit claim.

This process usually happens when a child is approaching the age of 16 (the age at which ordinarily they automatically become responsible for their own benefit claim). The parent often tells the Disability and Carers Service that they want to become an appointee for their child. Sometimes, though, the application is made when the young person is over the age of 16. When someone is made an appointee for an adult, the Department for Work and Pensions will send an officer to visit. The visit is simply to check that the appointee understands what the appointment involves, to make sure there is no financial abuse and to check that the young person is unable to manage their own benefit claim.

Future (education, employment, independent living)

People with autism and their needs vary greatly; so, therefore, does the support which they will require as they grow up and move into adulthood. There are many people with ASC who require little in the way of extra support, but many require some. This chapter is aimed at those who will need extra support.

Education, Health and Care Plan (EHCP)

If your child has an EHCP, this can stay with them up to the age of 25. The focus as your child becomes an adult will be on giving them the skills and support they need to become as independent as they can be in terms of self-care, living, education and employment. This means that the local authority (LA) will have an ongoing duty to arrange appropriate education, health and care support for your child. This should help to provide you with clear advice on what support is available to your child.

Post-16 education and training

Children in England must stay in education or training until they are 18 years old. This can be done alongside paid or voluntary work. At the age of 16, your child becomes a 'young person', and as such they have the right to decide what their next step in education or training will be. There is plenty of choice out there. Your young person could choose from the following:

- Remaining at the school they're at or going to another school
- Further Education college
- An apprenticeship
- A supported internship
- A programme of training and work experience

Just like at other transition points, it's vitally important to find out as much as you can about what the options entail and what might be best for your young person. Staff at your child's school will be able to help with this, and so might the LA's SEN department.

Extra support

Schools and colleges must ensure that they are supporting students with SEN. They have to adhere to the SEND Code of Practice (2017) (see page 119). The school or college will have a member of staff responsible for ensuring the provision for SEN students meets their needs. They may be called the SENCo, Learning Support Manager or something similar. Before making a decision on whether to apply for a place, I would recommend speaking to whoever is in charge of SEN provision.

Employment

The statistics for adults with autism in full-time paid employment are depressing – just 16%. However, there are signs that things are changing. People with ASC have many traits which are highly valuable in the workplace and some employers are starting to realise this. This has led to many companies actively seeking applicants with ASC for positions.

In addition, schemes such as supported employment (see below), which helps people with disabilities to secure and retain paid employment, may help people with ASC gain the skills they need to work.

Social skills

Starting in a job opens up all sorts of new and different social interactions and for some people with ASC this can be problematic. They may need to share a workspace, communicate clearly, make new friendships, network and any number of other potentially difficult things. There are also often unwritten social rules (e.g. tea break etiquette, staff rooms, socialising outside of the workplace) which go hand in hand with having a job. Again, this can prove problematic for some.

While in schools, there is generally an awareness of the needs of those with ASC and support is provided; this is not always the same in workplaces. However, if you think this may be a problem for your child as they get a job, you can encourage them to speak to their employer's HR department, who may be able to make some adjustments for them such as providing a workplace mentor.

It would also be a good idea to prepare your child for some of the unwritten rules of the workplace, governing things such as offering to make drinks for colleagues when you make one for yourself.

Workplace assessments

Employers can get a workplace assessment from the National Autistic Society for an employee with ASC who they feel would benefit from extra support.

Supported employment

Supported employment is a way of providing assistance to people with a disability to help them work, or help them gain the skills to work. At the heart of the model is the idea that anyone who wants paid employment can be employed if the right support is given. The scheme supports people looking for employment and also potential employers, and then matches employees and employers. More details can be found on the British Association for Supported Employment website (www.base-uk.org).

Independent living

If you have concerns about your child's ability to live independently and without any support as they move into adulthood, a care needs assessment by social services will be able to help determine the type of care that might be most applicable, and how this is to be funded.

There are many options for those who may find living completely independently difficult, such as:

- **Residential care**
  Residential homes give residents the chance to use some independent living skills (such as shopping and cooking) but provide support from staff. Residential homes are usually staffed 24 hours a day and must be registered, meeting certain requirements.

- **Supported living schemes**
  These schemes provide support to help people with disabilities live independently. The level and type of support they might receive is dependent on their needs. They aim to develop independent living skills in a safe, supportive environment. This may be in your own home, or in a property where the care provider is the landlord.

- **Shared lives schemes**
  Shared lives is similar to fostering, designed to make it easier for adults who might have difficulty living on their own. The schemes

match an adult with care needs with an approved shared lives carer. The carer supports and gives care to the adult with needs, and also shares their family and community life.

- **Homeshare**

  This is a scheme that enables two people who are unrelated to share a home for mutual benefit. Essentially it brings together two people who have different needs, who may be able to mutually benefit each other (e.g. providing care, helping around the house, providing companionship). It is a low-cost arrangement.

- **Care from family**

  Whether they live with you or close by, your child may benefit from ongoing help from you and other family members to support themselves.

Other forms of support

There are other forms of support which may help an adult with ASC in their daily life:

- **Day centres**

  A place to meet, socialise and do activities.

- **Outreach workers**

  The National Autistic Society has an outreach service to help people with ASC access opportunities and activities outside their home. This can include helping someone to attend a college course, to participate in a sport or hobby or to socialise.

- **Respite care**

  If someone is being cared for by their family, both them and their family may be eligible for a break away from each other. (See page 108 for more on this topic.)

is for

Genius

While I was researching this book, one parent told me of an encounter with a stranger. When she had explained to the stranger that her daughter had Asperger syndrome (AS), the reply was, 'Oh, lucky you – you have a genius. What's her special skill?'

You may also have heard something similar in your time. Because to a lot of people, autism is a byword for genius. But in reality, assuming someone is a genius because they have ASC is a bit like assuming that someone is a great footballer simply because they were born in Brazil.

Blame Hollywood

Part of the reason the general public often assumes that people with autism are geniuses is that this is a common trait for people with ASC in films, books and television shows. In *Rain Man*, Dustin Hoffman plays Raymond Babbitt, an autistic savant (someone who displays skills which are well beyond what is considered normal, but may have deficits in other areas) who has astonishing powers of recall and calculation. It's probably one of the most well-known portrayals of someone with autism, and has become shorthand for 'autistic savant'.

Similarly, the character Lisbeth Salander in *The Girl with the Dragon Tattoo* (and the rest of the *Millenium* series) is possibly the best computer hacker in the world, with a photographic memory. She enjoys nothing better than solving complex mathematical problems to unwind. While she doesn't have a diagnosis of ASC or AS in the book, author Stieg Larsson leaves a lot of clues that she has ASC – her incredible focus on the task at hand, her difficulty with social situations, her somewhat restricted diet. On his website, Larsson explained that he made the decision not to give Salander a diagnosis, so that readers saw her as a rounded character rather than just a diagnosis.

Books and TV shows also have a lot of characters with either suspected or diagnosed ASC. Some of the time, these characters are portrayed as geniuses in some way or other (e.g. Sheldon in *The Big Bang Theory*).

It's fair to say, though, that there are plenty of instances where characters with autism are not portrayed as geniuses in films and books, and that portrayal is becoming more widespread and varied.

Is the autistic genius a myth?

Certainly not. It is thought that a lot of geniuses in recent history might have been diagnosed with ASC if they had lived in this day and age. Some have suggested that scientists such as Albert Einstein, Sir Isaac Newton and Charles Darwin may have had autism. Similarly, others have hypothesised that Michelangelo and Mozart may also have been autistic. Although it can never be proven that someone who lived and died a long time ago had autism, it is worth noting that many of the things which helped these people to be geniuses in their fields are traits associated with autism, such as having an excellent working memory, attention to detail, intense concentration, a need for order and highly specialised and detailed knowledge of their specialist area. Renowned naturalist and presenter of *Springwatch*, Chris Packham, recently revealed that he has been diagnosed with AS. The animal behavioural professor, Temple Grandin – who has become something of a spokesperson for autism – also has a diagnosis of autism.

> A lot of geniuses in recent history might have been diagnosed with ASC if they had lived in this day and age.

Oh your child has Asperger's Syndrome. How wonderful. He must be a genius. What's his special skill?

But most people with ASC aren't geniuses... and that's okay

Most people with ASC are not geniuses, just like most neurotypical people are not geniuses. Rather than thinking that because your child has ASC they should be a genius, it might be more helpful to look at it the other way round – if your child is a genius, they more than likely also have traits of autism.

Girls

Okay, here is a shocking fact for you: 0% of the children I have educated have been girls with ASC. 100% of those with ASC have been boys. Yes, that's right – although I've been teaching in mainstream primary schools for almost twenty years, I have never taught a girl with autism in that time. Not one.

And I'd say that my experience is far from unique. Up and down the country, probably all around the world, there will be teachers like me who have never taught a girl with diagnosed ASC. Except of course, this fact doesn't really tell the truth. I don't believe for a second that none of the girls I've taught have had ASC. It would be more accurate to say that none of them have had a diagnosis. And that, according to the statistics, is also not a surprise. Estimates of the ratio of males to females with autism vary wildly, from 2:1 up to 15:1. But at present, girls are much less likely to be diagnosed with ASC than boys.

But why?

For a start, it's thought that girls with ASC are much better at hiding their symptoms than boys. To get an ASC diagnosis, children must be impaired in three areas: social imagination and flexibility of thought, social and emotional interaction, and social communication and language – the triad of impairments (see page 155). Girls, it seems, often manage pretty successfully to mask their difficulties with social situations. They do this by watching and learning from others, and therefore (superficially) it seems they're getting on okay. They may even have some friendships.

However, they might have some difficulty deviating from routine in school, getting anxious when things change. While a boy with ASC might be more likely to act out in school when anxious though (e.g. turning tables or hitting out), girls with undiagnosed ASC often come across as shy. Rather than act out, they frequently turn inward, internalising their anxiety. And this is how they slip under the radar. Their meltdowns are regularly left for home.

Two sides to every story

While a girl with ASC might manage to keep a lid on all that anxiety while she's at school and behave perfectly, it is common for the undesirable behaviours to bubble over at home instead. Often, teachers don't even realise this is what

> **It's thought that girls with ASC are much better at hiding their symptoms than boys.**

is going on at home. And this can make it difficult for parents to get their concerns taken seriously by professionals. I've known many parents who have girls who have 'coped' at school, but had real issues with behaviour and anxiety at home. When parents have looked into this and suspected ASC, they've often been told by doctors that the issue is a parenting one because the symptoms aren't present at school.

However, those who manage to convince their GP and secure a referral for an ASC assessment can also find difficulties. When the referral is accepted, forms are usually sent to both the parents and school, so they can give their views on the strengths and difficulties of the young person. This can be a stumbling block if the girl's symptoms aren't obvious in school. The evidence that the school provides to the process can often be insufficient and prevent the case from going ahead to a full assessment, despite the parents' forms showing there is an issue at home.

Even if you negotiate the first two hurdles of referral and forms, the assessment itself can also prove to be inconclusive for girls. As girls are much more likely to mask their difficulties, it isn't unusual for them to hide them from the professionals when they complete their part of the assessment. This will mean they'll come out with a more even profile for social skills and the team might not be able to reach a diagnosis of ASC.

So it isn't a level playing field for boys and girls?

In short, no it isn't. Aside from it being more difficult to get referred for an assessment, the diagnostic criteria for ASC are based on the behavioural characteristics of men and boys on the autism spectrum. Logically, this means that the current diagnostic criteria are much better at picking out males on the spectrum than females. Girls continue to fall through the net. However, understanding about girls and autism is growing all the time. Let's hope that before long, this will result in a set of criteria which are set up to more accurately assess girls as well as boys.

So what can I do?

Persevere

If you strongly suspect that your daughter has ASC but you're struggling to get your concerns heard, don't stop trying. There are hundreds, thousands, of others out there who had to struggle through to eventually get heard. The professionals who turn you away aren't always proven to be right. In the course of writing this book, nearly every parent I've spoken with has had to show perseverance to get the right diagnosis and/ or support for their children, few more so than parents of girls with ASC.

In an ideal world, the world of ASC and SEN would not be one where those who shout the loudest and longest get the most support, but on occasion, that's what it is.

Use the strategies anyway

A diagnosis is nothing more than a label. It is useful only in that it highlights your child's needs to others. The strategies that will help your child to make the most of life, to feel more comfortable in social situations and to ease anxiety are available to all. Use them at home and try to encourage school to do the same.

Get the professionals on your side

You will stand a much better chance of getting referred if you can get the professionals on your side. Speak to your child's teacher and SENCo about your concerns. If you're in a position where the behaviours are shown at home more than in school, make sure you communicate this to the school. If you can convince them, they'll be able to make the referral themselves. You may also need to convince your GP.

Do your research

If you're knocked back by any of the professionals because there is a discrepancy between how your daughter behaves at school and home, show them some of the research that shows this is common in girls with ASC. Even by simply typing 'girls and ASC' into a search engine, you'll be able to find enough evidence to back you up.

Keep a record of behaviours

This could be important if your daughter's issues show up most readily at home, rather than at school. Having a record of what has happened will help to show school staff, your GP and others the exact nature of your daughter's difficulties.

CASE STUDY

Abigail

Our daughter Abigail wasn't diagnosed until she was twelve years old. Up until six months before diagnosis, we'd not even suspected that she could be autistic.

But looking back – as we had to do during the assessment – it was obvious that the signs were there, if you looked hard enough. Abigail had hit her milestones pretty much as expected – talking, walking, potty training etc. In fact, she'd been a little precocious with her ability to talk. She was talking in long, complex sentences not long after her first birthday. She was like a magpie in the way she would pick up words and phrases from the adults around her. Sometimes, she'd get these long words and complicated phrases kind of mixed up, but often they'd be used correctly. We thought we were just particularly good at this parenting business.

Abigail's great love was books. Still is (well, that and Youtube). She soon learned all of her picture books by heart, knowing which words went with which pictures. By eighteen months of age, Abigail would sit herself down with her pile of picture books and amuse herself for an hour or more, 'reading' to herself. Later, when she was four or five, she would choose to play with her fairy books, rather than her teddies or any of the other toys we'd bought. She'd line them up in rows on her bedroom floor, telling each one of them what she'd like them to do in the game. When she played with her younger siblings, she'd do the same, telling them exactly where to stand and what to say and do in the game.

But it was when she mixed with other children that we really noticed Abigail was different to them because, while her friends at toddler group all played with one another, Abigail would simply stand and watch them, trying to make sense of what was going on. When she did play, Abigail preferred to play with just one other friend. We just assumed she was shy. There are a few people in the family who could be considered shy, myself included.

It was a similar story when she started nursery. Abigail didn't cry when we left her there or when we picked her up. But staff reported back to us that she would stand and watch the other children as they played, rarely joining in, and that she would need a lot of preparing for when anything out of the ordinary routine was going to happen.

She made it through primary school. Every parents' evening, we'd be told that she was very shy, that she had just one or two good friends, that she was almost too well behaved and that she was achieving beyond expectations for her year group. No-one ever mentioned autism.

It was when she started secondary school that things really started to fall apart. A couple of months in, we started to experience meltdowns at home. It started with her refusing to come on a car journey with the rest of the family to meet friends. To begin with, she was just defiant. Then she started swearing. And after that she became violent. It was the most shocking, unexpected thing we'd experienced. Out of nowhere, our daughter seemed to have developed into an angry little demon. She would follow us around the house, swearing and threatening us. It was a very tough time indeed. We asked our GP for help. They referred us to Child and Adolescent Mental Health Services (CAMHS). But we heard nothing. It wasn't until she'd threatened to kill either herself or us with knives that her case was accelerated and we were seen by CAMHS. After seeing Abigail for a little while (during which time her anxiety and behaviour stabilised), the psychotherapist suggested that our daughter's difficulties could possibly be linked to autism. She had noticed a rigidity in Abigail's behaviour and thinking. She referred us on.

And all of a sudden it was like someone had turned the lights on. We started to look back over Abigail's childhood to date and realised that some of the things that we had taken as shyness might have another context.

We went to the assessment and gave our side of the story. Abigail went into another room to complete her part of the assessment. A little later, at the feedback meeting, they explained that although the parental interview indicated autism, Abigail's assessment indicated otherwise. It was borderline. They came down on the side of no diagnosis. But then they told us what Abigail had said in her interview. She'd led them to believe that she had a wide group of friends who she would frequently go shopping with at weekends. This wasn't the truth. They assessed her again and this time reached a diagnosis of ASC – unofficially Asperger syndrome.

J *is for*

Jargon

Being a parent of a child with ASC doesn't come with a dictionary. It should. Even before you've reached diagnosis you'll have been bombarded with jargon and acronyms.

ADOS. The spectrum. ASD. ASC. SALT. AS. SEN. IEP. The triad of impairments. Annual review. SEND. Community Paediatrician. OT. Social Communication. PECS. Social stories. EP. Comic strip conversations. PDA. Stimming. EHCP. Sensory integration. PDD. M-CHAT. SENCo. The list could go on. And on. And on.

These words and plenty more will be flung around, often without explanation, and you'll be expected to know what they mean. More often than not you'll be first introduced to these words by one of the many professionals your child has worked with. They'll fire off the words at high speed in the middle of a sentence that it seems vital you understand. If you're lucky, they'll interpret the slightly baffled and worried expression on your face and they'll slow down, explaining each new term as they use it. If you're brave, maybe you'll stop them in their tracks and ask them to explain in words that you've heard before.

> **Being a parent of a child with ASC doesn't come with a dictionary. It should.**

If you find yourself in this type of situation, try not to judge. Chances are that no-one is trying to bamboozle you. Those of us involved in education, SEN and health like to make sure you understand what we're talking about, but sometimes we just forget ourselves. We get so used to using these terms and acronyms that sometimes we forget that not everybody is fluent in our gibberish language. (Plus, sometimes we feel so busy that we think we don't even have time to slow our sentences down.)

There's not much you can do to prepare yourself for the jargon and the acronyms. It is like learning a new language (although much less fun). Don't think you'll look silly by asking people to slow down, to repeat themselves or explain what they really mean. It's their job to help you and your children, so you'll be helping them to do their job more effectively. Most of the jargon you'll come across will be explained somewhere in this book. You'll also find a glossary of acronyms on page 161. You'll find definitions of any that I've missed (or that have been invented since I wrote this!) by typing them into a search engine and pressing enter.

Medication

There is no cure for autism, as discussed on page 34. However, some people with a diagnosis of autism are prescribed medication to help treat some of the associated and/or co-existing conditions, such as:

- **Depression** (treated with selective serotonin reuptake inhibitors (SSRIs))
- **Sleep problems** (treated with drugs like melatonin)
- **Epilepsy** (treated with anti-convulsant drugs)
- **ADHD** (there are five kinds of drugs sometimes prescribed for ADHD, including methylphenidate, which don't cure ADHD but can help children to concentrate better)
- **Challenging behaviour** (anti-psychotic drugs can be prescribed, if other treatments haven't worked or the behaviour is severe)

Side effects

All of these medications have associated side effects and are available only on prescription. You will therefore need to see a medical professional before your child can take any.

My child refuses to take medication, though

Some children with ASC don't like to take medication and this can become an issue. There are a few tactics you can employ to help.
My first stop would be to explain the benefit of the medication to them. It might be enough to simply do this verbally. Alternatively, you could use a social story to help.

It might also be worth doing some detective work into what it is that your child doesn't like about taking the medication – for instance, it could be the taste or it could be that they find swallowing caplets or tablets difficult. Once you have worked this out, you may be able to find a version of the medication which your child can take in a form they are more likely to cope with. If not, you should at least know what the issue is.

If your child has to regularly take medication, you may be able to use routine to get them to take it. Having an incentive may work for some children (e.g. 'if you take your tablet now, you can have a square of chocolate after').

If none of these things work, you may need to see if you can hide the medication inside something that they will like, such as a smoothie.

Meetings

There will be meetings. Tens of them. Possibly even hundreds of them.

There will be meetings to discuss concerns. Meetings to discuss progress. Meetings to organise assessments. Meetings where you'll be asked to repeat the same developmental history as you have already done a million times before. Meetings about behaviour. Meetings about funding. Meetings about support. Meetings about changes to school provision. Meetings about meetings.

Sometimes the meetings will be filled with professionals with impressive but intimidating job titles and you'll want the world to open up and swallow you. Other times there will be meetings where you're desperate for those same professionals to show their face, and they won't. Don't get me wrong, meetings can be wonderful (okay, maybe that's an exaggeration). They can be the place where things get decided, where you ensure that everyone is singing from the same metaphorical hymn sheet and getting things right for your child. But they can also be a source of enormous stress for parents.

Most parents start with the disadvantage that they are inexperienced in these type of meetings. The other attendees will usually be education, health or social care professionals who get paid for attending meetings exactly like yours, and they'll have been to hundreds of them before. They know what the jargon means. They speak at a million miles an hour. And what's more, they're usually very busy and need to get to the next meeting. Sometimes it can feel to the parent that the professionals had their minds made up on the outcome of a meeting before they even stepped through the door and they hold the power to decide *yes* or *no*. And in such circumstances, it isn't unknown for parents to reach the end of the meeting feeling like a rabbit transfixed by the headlights of an oncoming lorry. Their voice doesn't get heard. It feels like they were invited as little more than a courtesy, rather than as an active member.

It's can seem massively unfair. The professional has little at stake in the meeting (other than perhaps adding to their workload) whereas for you and your child, the outcome of this meeting could be vital. So, here are a few tips to help redress the balance of power back in your favour.

> Meetings can be a source of enormous stress for parents.

Top tips for successful, stress-free meetings

Forewarned is forearmed

Get prepared for the meeting. Try to find out its purpose before you attend. Either contacting the person organising the meeting or a quick internet search will give you some insight into what the meeting will be about.

Eyes on the prize

Think through what you want to get from the meeting before you go. Making some notes would be a good idea.

Go armed with evidence

Before you're far along the path of ASC and SEN, you'll probably have enough experience and enough reports on your child to be able to take plenty of information to the meeting with you.

Don't take it personally

Easier said than done, I realise. But sometimes you might be told things you don't want to hear. Sometimes you might feel like your parenting skills are being questioned. Sometimes the focus of a meeting will be on what your child *can't* do, rather than what they *can* do. Try to take a step back from the situation and evaluate what you're being told. Is it helpful to your child and the support they'll get? Or is it something you need to take issue with?

Moral support

Whoever is organising the meeting should be fine with you taking someone with you. A little moral support can help you feel more confident to say your piece. It could be a family member, a friend or an advocate.

Speak up

If it feels like your presence is little more than a token gesture and you have something to say, make sure you get a chance to say it. You are the number one most important person in your young person's life and vice versa – you should get a say.

Expert advice

If you have a grievance or would like extra, independent support and advice in a meeting, get in touch with your local authority (LA) Parent Partnership SEN Support Worker (note that they may have a different job title in your LA). If you're not sure who they are, check out the LA's website. They can offer independent support and advice on the processes, legalities and practicalities of anything SEN. They will help fight your corner in meetings.

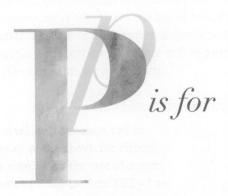

P *is for*

Parents

Parenthood is one of the most amazing experiences on Earth. But it can sometimes feel like being strapped into a rollercoaster – full of exhilarating highs and knuckle-whitening lows, with a few stomach-churning moments thrown in for good measure. The same can be said for all parents, but for parents of children with ASC, very often the highs are higher and the lows are lower (and the stomach-churning moments are... erm... churnier).

> **Parents often tend to bear the brunt of their child's behaviour.**

Taking the strain

Being a parent has a high workload; there are many demands on your time. These demands may be greater for a parent of a child with ASC than for the average parent.

Appointments

Let's start with the number of appointments, meetings and assessments you may be asked to attend. There will be a lot of meetings, and sometimes they will be stressful. What's more, you may find that you need to negotiate with work or find childcare to allow you to attend the meetings in the first place. While some appointments and meetings may not be easily moved to fit in with your schedule, it is always worth asking if a meeting can be scheduled to suit you.

Information overload

Most parents of children with ASC will also be put on a very steep learning curve. There is a lot to find out about ASC and SEN. It is easy to feel that you don't know enough or that you could be doing more. The amount of information that comes your way may seem overwhelming. Don't be afraid to ask if there is something you don't understand or don't know.

Behaviour

One of the biggest challenges to family life, your sanity and your relationships, is that you, as a parent, will tend to bear the brunt of your child's behaviour. Plus, unlike a teacher or a teaching assistant, your shift never really ends. This can make family life really tough. Dealing with violent or difficult behaviour has a big impact on all those in and around the family home – parents, siblings, other relatives, friends, even pets – for a number of different reasons. For instance, it can place you in actual physical danger (you'd be amazed – or maybe you wouldn't – at the number of parents that end up having to call the police to help resolve situations with their own children). It can also drive a wedge between members of the family; for example, siblings can be confused about the seemingly different sets of rules which apply to them and their sibling with ASC. If this is an area which is causing stress for your family, make sure you seek help from an appropriate professional (you might try speaking to your child's school, Child and Adolescent Mental Health Services (CAMHS) or your GP), or from other parents who have been through similar experiences.

Attitudes of others

I've covered this in the section on bad parenting (see page 17), but it's worth reiterating here that it is likely that as a parent of a child with ASC, you will be subject to the unwelcome opinions of others – parents in the playground and on the school run, random strangers in the supermarket, even family members and friends. While you'll also find the world is full of plenty of people who will be supportive and understanding, it's those that aren't that tend to stick in the memory. These are the ones that make you doubt yourself, that make you think you're doing the wrong things for your child. If you let them get to you, you may find yourself changing your behaviours and routines to suit them. Don't. Seek help instead – if it's happening at school, contact the Special Educational Needs Coordinator (SENCo) or headteacher. If you're not sure how to tackle the problem, join a support group – there will be people there who have been through the same things you're facing.

Relationship strain

Let's be frank, relationships can be tested by all of the above. It's difficult to put a number on the rate of divorce for parents of children with ASC – I've seen it reported at anything from 40% (roughly the UK average of 42%) up to 90% (though this figure is generally thought to be a myth with no evidence or source).

> It may be that you could be eligible for some respite, which will give you some time away from caring.

But it doesn't need to be this way. There are many couples who find that their relationship or marriage is strengthened by having a child with ASC. Your relationship is also really important in bringing up your child. If your relationship works well, you'll be able to deal with the highs and lows of parenting a child with ASC – when one parent is feeling low, the other steps in. If you feel that your relationship is being put under extra pressure because of your child's needs, you'd be well advised to speak to someone like a social worker. It may be that you could be eligible for some respite, which will give you some time away from caring.

Pathological demand avoidance (PDA)

Let's be honest, if a child didn't try to avoid doing something they disliked, if they always happily obeyed commands, we'd be a little concerned. It's quite normal for children to want to negotiate, to gain control, to make their needs and wants known. A little push back from children (and adults) is sometimes a healthy thing. But for some, avoiding doing what other people ask seems to go to extremes.

PDA is a fairly controversial area of autism (yep, another one). In this case, it's because PDA isn't recognised as a diagnosis of its own. In the past, someone presenting with the traits of PDA may have been diagnosed with atypical autism – maybe Asperger syndrome or pervasive developmental disorder not otherwise specified. At present, they're most likely to be given the catch-all diagnosis of ASC. Indeed, if you seek a diagnosis of PDA, more likely than not, you'll be told it doesn't exist. As simple as that.

However, the way a child on the spectrum presents and the way a child with a behaviour profile of PDA presents can be very different. More importantly, the strategies which might successfully be employed to help a child with PDA are very different (almost the inverse) of those typically used to help children with ASC. So I think PDA deserves a chapter of its own.

So what is PDA?

The main outward sign that your child may have a profile of PDA is that they avoid everyday demands and expectations, almost as if they're driven to do so. Often, this can be through quite extreme behaviour (e.g. trashing rooms, hitting and kicking). At other times, it can look like the child is extremely good at manipulating situations and people, as they seem to gain control in every situation.

> The way a child on the spectrum presents and the way a child with a behaviour profile of PDA presents can be very different.

You see, really, control is the point. Someone with a behaviour profile of PDA behaves in the way that they do so they can gain some control of a situation. This is borne of anxiety at the idea that demands will be placed on them. So, in order to either avoid a situation or feel in control of it, the child will employ a variety of strategies to derail the demand or gain some control over what is about to be asked of them.

For instance, a child might always become extremely anxious at the thought of being asked to write. He might be sitting in a lesson, answering questions, smiling and joking with the rest of the class. But as soon as it becomes clear that today's task is to write using just paper and pencil, the child will employ a range of strategies to avoid having to do it. It might start with a high-pitched whining noise. From there, it might move onto protests: 'I don't want to do this', 'I don't know what to do', or even 'my arm doesn't work'. The last stage is often physical – upending furniture, hitting, hiding under tables, throwing things. Demand successfully avoided.

How will I know if my child has PDA?

As I mentioned before, getting a diagnosis of PDA is tricky. However, if your child regularly shows or has shown many of the following behaviours, it might be worth considering whether they have a profile of PDA.

- Avoids or resists the demands of everyday life
- Sometimes avoids doing even those things that they like doing when asked
- Uses avoidance strategies (e.g. gives excuses, distracts, negotiates, time-wastes, has physical outbursts, withdraws into fantasy, argues, physically incapacitates themselves (e.g. says 'my legs don't work'))
- Can have meltdowns (throws, kicks, shouts, screams, hits)
- May become more resistant to demand as they grow older
- Can seem manipulative and controlling
- Changes avoidance strategies for different people
- Struggles to see boundaries (e.g. doesn't see why a child shouldn't be able to do what an adult does)
- Can become overfamiliar or bossy with adults
- May like to be spoken to like an adult
- Appears to have good communication and to be sociable, but actually lacks social understanding
- May understand non-verbal communication to a greater extent than others on the autism spectrum
- Can be polite
- Is able to roleplay and pretend play
- Can be impulsive
- May seem uninhibited (i.e. lacks pride or embarrassment)
- Can experience mood swings
- Has a passive early history – some milestones may be missed
- Has language delay, but possibly with a rapid catch up
- Shows obsessive behaviour, sometimes about other people
- May struggle to take responsibility for own actions

- Can be unpredictable
- Likes to be in charge of games and play, without taking the needs of others into account
- Has sensory processing difficulties

How to get assessed

This is where it gets complicated. At the time of writing, PDA is not recognised by the DSM-V or ICD-10 (the two main diagnostic criteria for psychiatric assessment). This means that getting a diagnosis of PDA is difficult.

That isn't to say it's impossible, though. To begin with, if you feel that your child may have a behaviour profile which matches PDA, speak to a professional – perhaps your GP or the school's Special Educational Needs Coordinator (SENCo). If they agree with you, they might agree to make a referral for you. In most cases this would be either to Child and Adolescent Mental Health Services (CAMHS) or a paediatrician.

More than likely, though, if there is no existing diagnosis your child will be diagnosed with something like ASC or oppositional defiance disorder. If you already have a diagnosis of ASC but you feel a diagnosis of PDA might be a better fit, be prepared that you may be knocked back at any of the above stages. I've spoken to many parents about this subject and have heard many times that they've been advised not to go for a diagnosis. One parent told me that they'd even been advised that getting the diagnosis would result in less support for their child. And in my role as a SENCo, when I have referred to CAMHS asking for an assessment of PDA, I've received a reply saying that it doesn't exist and that the case is closed.

The case doesn't necessarily need to be closed though. The Elizabeth Newson Centre in Nottingham specialises in PDA. But to get an assessment from the centre, you'll need to either fund it yourself or convince your local authority or NHS trust that this is something worth investigating. Once again, this could be a postcode lottery.

And if you find yourself frustrated in your quest for a diagnosis, don't be downhearted. Even in the absence of a diagnosis, if your child has an Education, Health and Care Plan (EHCP) you could try to get it altered so that it clearly reflects someone with a profile of PDA rather than simply ASC, even if PDA is never mentioned. This should help to make sure that your child gets the right provision in school.

As with most conditions, the way you respond, the strategies you put in place and the adjustments you make are always of much greater worth than the diagnosis itself. No-one can take the strategies away from you, even if they're not willing to recognise PDA as a separate condition of its own. And that's where the next section will come in handy.

The useful stuff: strategies

Many of the strategies which normally work well for children on the autism spectrum may only have limited success (if that) with a child who has PDA. Many of the strategies for people with ASC revolve around providing a structure and preparing the child for what is about to happen. However, this structured approach can be too inflexible for children who present with a behavioural profile of PDA. They will need things to be a lot more flexible and the demands placed on them will need to be less directive, and instead have an element of choice or control.

> The demands placed on the child will need to have an element of choice or control.

What you will be aiming to do is negate the anxiety that the child feels.

But this can be tricky. I've known children who are so driven to avoid demands that they will even turn down the things that they really like, just so they can control the situation. This can make it really difficult to anticipate how they will react to the situation you present them with. It may also mean that something that works once won't necessarily work the next time you try it. Here are some tips to get you started.

Be flexible

You'll need to be prepared to change the best laid plans at a moment's notice. This doesn't always mean abandoning them though. In school, we always think of what we want the end outcome to be and then work backwards to see how we can accomplish that without causing anxiety. For instance, if we want the child to learn about converting measurements between grams and kilos, we know that presenting this information in the form of the worksheet the rest of the class is doing will most likely cause a battle which we will lose. So instead we'll look at fun ways of doing the work – practical approaches work well, as do exercises to identify where someone else has gone wrong. This means a lot of forward planning. It can be exhausting. But the positive impact on both you and the child is immense.

Chop and change your strategies

So you've finally found a strategy that works! You've tried it again and it worked the second time too. Hooray! Time to rejoice. You can pat yourself on the back and go into the next similar situation confident that you have something that will do the job. Oh... but what's this? Your child has very quickly got wise to your strategy and it no longer works. Drat. Welcome to the world of demand avoidance.

Unfortunately, that scenario is not uncommon. As soon as the child realises that they've been hoodwinked into doing something they didn't want to do, they'll feel that they've lost control and look to gain it again. And that means your strategy has probably had its day.

So what to do? Well, I'd advise developing a bag of tricks, which you can chop and change so they don't become predictable. Again, this can be pretty exhausting.

Try novel approaches

So, with the above in mind, here are some practical ideas:

- Try to create mystery and suspense.
- Plan what you do around the child's interests.
- Try to involve activities which the child will think are fun.
- Use drama.
- Try to give a real-life context to activities.
- Act like the idiot who can't quite get it right – kids with PDA love to point out when adults have got it wrong.

CASE STUDY

Ronny

I was called in to help with a pupil at our mainstream primary school who had a PDA-type profile. I took one look at the work expected to be completed in the lesson – a horrifically dull maths worksheet – and realised immediately that if I asked Ronny to do it, I'd have a meltdown to deal with. So I tried to think on my feet. I grabbed a marker pen and some post-it notes and hastily wrote the questions out. I posted the questions on the underneath of the table and then suggested that Ronny might like to have a go at answering them. Ronny immediately disappeared under the table and had the questions finished in no time at all. He also had a smile on his face.

Another time, another maths lesson and another dull worksheet, I needed to think outside the box. The worksheet in question was a list of addition sums, involving adding up items of food shopping. I realised that making the demand on Ronny might cause him anxiety, so instead I told him that I had done some shopping online at a supermarket, but that I thought they had got my bill wrong. I gave him the total I had paid and the list of items I had bought. Before I could blink, Ronny had logged onto the website, priced the items, added them up, compared the totals and calculated that I'd been overcharged by £4.58. He loved being able to prove someone wrong and enjoyed doing the activity without realising it was a maths task.

Use what motivates them

This is a pretty essential strategy for parenting any child. But for a child with a behaviour profile of PDA, using interests is especially important. If you can present things in a way which keys into their special interests, they're much more likely to want to comply. For instance, rather than trying to impose the topic of a project on a child, they are far more likely to enjoy working on (and thus learn more) if they can dictate the topic of their project themselves. This can be something important to talk to school about when approaching homework. If you have permission to be more flexible and use your child's interests to do homework, you could avert lots of stressful meltdowns and help your child achieve a lot more academically. For instance, if the class is tasked with writing an information text on the Victorians and you know your child will not comply, it might be best to change either the means of recording the information (making a video clip, for instance) or the subject (if your child loves trains, write an information text on that instead).

> If you can present things in a way which keys into their special interests, they're much more likely to want to comply.

There will be good days as well as bad

You'll soon be able to work out when you can push a little more and when you have to back off or be flexible.

Responsibility

Since children with PDA like to be in charge of the situation, this is something you can use to your (and their) advantage. For instance, we had a child with PDA and sensory regulating difficulties at school who didn't like to be asked to leave the classroom to go and take a learning break or do some occupational therapy exercises. We found that giving the child a responsibility – in this case, being in charge of making sure the sunflowers were watered and weeded – gave an excellent reason to get out of the classroom and gave the child some control.

Another example of this working well is the case of a child who would refuse to get into the school transport to go to school in the mornings. By offering them a responsibility once on board the transport – checking names off a list – the problem was resolved.

Negotiate

Sometimes this is a difficult one to accept as adults are usually the ones with the final say, but you'll soon realise that trying to impose your wishes on your child will just lead to greater anxiety and more behavioural outbursts. Instead, try negotiating.

Every day is a new day

Try not to let what has happened in the past colour what happens today. Start each day anew, full of opportunity to succeed. Easy to write in a book, but often more difficult when you're in the middle of a battle, I realise. But this is good advice that will help your child deal with their level of anxiety, and probably help you as a parent too.

Distraction

This can be a very useful tool to help with the de-escalation of meltdowns. Having a pack of age-appropriate distraction devices is a great idea. For younger children, we've used things like squeezy toys, things that light up,

> Try not to let what has happened in the past colour what happens today.

bubble mixture and bouncy balls. For older children, you might want to key into their interests – for instance, using books or comics. I've even known a meltdown averted when we noticed a wasp trying to get out of the window and attempted to help it.

Think about the way you phrase things

The way you phrase demands can have a great bearing on whether they get fulfilled or whether another meltdown becomes imminent. Direct commands are likely to increase anxiety, so try some of these ways of phrasing demands:

Use some reverse psychology. If you have a child who likes to prove you wrong, it may be worth phrasing your demand as a challenge.

It can also work to de-personalise the demands by using imaginary characters, visuals, cartoons and messages from others (e.g. a message from the headteacher asking the child to help with something).

Provide choice

This can be a good compromise as it can allow both the child and the adult an element of managed control of a situation. The way it works is that rather than presenting one option, the adult presents two or more ways for something to be done. The crucial thing from the child's point of view is that they get to choose which way they do it. From the adult's point of view, they also get to choose – they simply make sure that any of the suggested outcomes is acceptable to them.

Stay calm, be kind

It can be easy to get drawn into a battle with your child. Try not to. Take deep breaths. Step away. By doing this, you'll be able to respond more appropriately to their needs. You'll also give them time to calm down. And, even more importantly, you'll be modelling the best way for them to deal with anxiety – staying calm.

To begin with, you might view meltdowns as bad behaviour, as simple as that. But the more they happen, you will notice that the behaviour is a result of anxiety. Try treating each meltdown as an anxiety attack. You wouldn't try and shout someone out of an anxiety attack, would you? You'd try to calm them down, allow them space, and speak kindly and calmly.

Know your child

This sounds obvious and patronising, I realise. But the relationship and trust you build between you and your child is the most important thing. Knowing your child and having a positive relationship will help you to understand when to push and when not to pursue demands. It will also help your child trust that you won't ask them to do unreasonable things. The same should be true at school too – teachers, teaching assistants and any other adults who work with your child need to work hard at building and maintaining that relationship.

Take a break

It's also worth bearing in mind that sometimes adults will need a break – negotiating, pre-empting, carefully planning and staying calm when a meltdown arrives can be exhausting. If you can, share the load.

Keep ground rules to a minimum

But make sure those you do have are important and firm.

Avoid confrontation where possible

This can be done by thinking ahead and planning your approach some of the time. Other times (e.g. during meltdowns) you will need to stay calm and avoid debating the issue. Leave talking about issues that have arisen until later, when the child is calm.

Before

After   "But... How?"

"Easy. I told him that under no circumstances should he do his homework."

Provide a safe place

If your child experiences explosive behaviour, try having a den-like safe place where they can go to calm down. Give them space and time to compose themselves. This will also give you time to gather strength. A pop-up tent with cushions works well. Putting books or comics that they like or sensory toys into the den will give them something else to focus on, other than the anxiety which caused the behaviour.

Teach them how to cope with anxiety

Help your child develop strategies which reduce anxiety. A den (see above) can be a safe place and will reduce anxiety. You can also teach relaxation methods (e.g. using a relaxation CD, taking more physical exercise). An occupational therapist may be able to help with this by suggesting activities which promote movement and address any sensory issues.

Build self-esteem

Having a mentor – someone to show good work to, play games with, chat to etc – could be valuable. Many schools have Emotional Literacy Support Assistants who work with children on self-esteem and feelings. Ask your school what they can do to support this.

Use humour

Humour often works very well. Deployed well, it can often help to diffuse difficult situations. It also helps build trust and camaraderie and make life more enjoyable.

Use complex language in demands

Although this is the opposite of advice for most children with ASC, you may find it works well with children with a behaviour profile of PDA – it seems less child-like and is the language of negotiation, which will appeal to children with PDA.

Make sure the right professionals are involved

You should expect your child to have been seen by speech and language therapists, occupational therapists, educational psychologists, the school's SENCo, teaching assistants, local autism services, behaviour specialists, paediatricians and others too. If they haven't been, ask why.

CASE STUDY

Sandy

I know you're not supposed to compare your children, but that's what we did. At the age of two we realised that Sandy's speech and language was nowhere near as advanced as that of her sister at that age. The health visitor told us not to worry, that Sandy was young and that it would sort itself out. But we were concerned enough to self-refer to the speech and language service. From there, Sandy was referred to a paediatrician, who diagnosed her with ASC. We came out the other side of the meeting with a diagnosis, a leaflet and information about a support group.

It was at a support group for parents of girls with ASC that I noticed Sandy was different to the other children. I went searching for more information and discovered PDA, which more accurately described Sandy. I took this new information to the paediatrician, who told me there was not much point in saying she had PDA, as it wasn't recognised as a separate condition. However, the paediatrician wrote in a report that she had demand-avoidant behaviours. Later, we sought a diagnosis of PDA and were referred to the Great Ormond Street Hospital National Centre for High Functioning Autism. They worked with Sandy over the course of a year but during that time the diagnostic criteria changed, so they couldn't diagnose PDA.

Sandy is now in Year 5 at a mainstream primary school with an unfunded EHCP and one-to-one support provided by the school. They try to adapt to her needs and interests as much as they can. Being flexible is very important for Sandy. If you can approach learning through her own interests, it is much easier to get her engaged with a task. She says she just wants to go to a school which is fun.

At the beginning, we knew very little about ASC. It has been like playing a game with a blindfold on and without knowing the rules. Sometimes it has been exhausting, but support groups and blogging have helped me connect with other parents and they're the ones who always give the best advice!

Puberty (and sex and relationships)

Okay guys, take a seat. It's time we had a little talk, author to reader, about the... erm... you know, the birds and the... erm... well, the bees.

Okay, relax. I'm only joking. But we do need to talk about puberty and ASC.

Puberty is a time of massive change. Changes to the way your body looks. Changes to your hormones. Changes to what you like and what you don't like. Massive swings of emotion. And that's not to mention the sudden interest in things of a sexual nature that often arrives. As we know, for most children with ASC, change is difficult. So it stands to reason that puberty and adolescence can be a confusing and difficult time for young people with ASC.

I don't need to read this – they'll cover it all in sex education at school, won't they?

Yes, schools will teach about puberty, sex, sexuality and relationships. It's very probable though that a young person with ASC may need a little longer to take this information in, may need it reinforcing and explaining and perhaps may need a little more context. You might also find that your child with ASC will have a lot of questions about puberty (or they may refuse to talk about it point blank). Be prepared to answer any questions in as honest and straightforward a way as you can. You may occasionally get asked a question which you need to check the answer to before giving it. This is absolutely fine.

Give it to me straight

Historically, talking about puberty, sex and sexuality (especially with one's own children) has been seen as difficult and people have turned to euphemism and metaphor to help them explain – the birds and the bees would be the prime example. As a society we're moving slowly away from this culture, but there are still phrases which stick around which might be confusing or alarming to a child with ASC, such as someone's voice 'breaking'. People with ASC tend to find non-literal language confusing, so it is important to stick to the facts. You may also find that your child wants answers that are medically or scientifically accurate. If you're not sure of an answer, don't be afraid to tell your child that you will check it and get back to them.

Be prepared to answer any questions in as honest and straightforward a way as you can.

Smells like teen spirit

It is important to prepare your child for physical changes that will happen as they grow older and enter puberty. Let's start with the smelly stuff. Deodorant – and personal hygiene – will suddenly become a must for your child. But your child might not realise this, particularly if they have sensory differences. It can be a tricky subject to broach for any parent. If you have difficulty convincing your child that washing more often and using a deodorant is a good idea, I'd suggest using a social story to help as you may need to explain the social conventions around personal hygiene.

A close shave

As with smells, you may also need to explain the social conventions around shaving. You'll probably also need to teach your child how to shave and if they have difficulties either with motor skills or following instructions, be prepared to supervise.

Periods

Your daughter may need some reassurance about menstruation; that it's entirely normal, that she won't bleed to death. You should also show her how to use sanitary products and discuss what she should do if her period comes when she is at school – for instance, who to go to. A social story may help with this to begin with. Once your daughter has started her periods, you can also help her to understand her monthly cycle and when her next period is likely to arrive, so she is well prepared when it does.

You'll go blind

You will probably also want to talk about masturbation (okay, you probably won't want to, but you might need to). An awkward and embarrassing conversation might help pre-empt infinitely more awkward situations later on! It's important for your child to understand that masturbation is completely healthy and normal. It's also important that they know it's something that should be done in private – you may need to identify where might be an appropriate place and agree that if a bedroom or bathroom door is closed, people should knock and wait before entering.

Relationships (romantic and platonic)

As discussed elsewhere in this book, social interaction is often an area of difficulty for children with ASC and they may need help making and maintaining friendships. The same is true when children with ASC reach adolescence and start to think about relationships. They may have difficulties understanding the difference between different types of friendships and relationships, and this could be an area you need to broach with them. You may also need to discuss boundaries – understanding their own and other people's. Some people with ASC also find the idea of intimacy (such as kissing and hugging another person) difficult. Using strategies like comic strip conversations and social stories may help with many of these problems.

R is for

Rejecting a diagnosis

Not everyone is happy to receive a diagnosis of ASC. In fact, it isn't unknown for people to reject their diagnosis outright. Quite often, it may be that the family is in denial that their child has ASC. But it is also sometimes the case that children start to question their diagnosis and disown it.

Why do parents reject a diagnosis?

For many reasons. Rejecting a diagnosis is more common than you might think. For many parents, it can take a long time to accept that their child has any difficulties. Sometimes this might be because their child is a borderline case, who only just meets the threshold for diagnosis. Sometimes it is because the child is their oldest and they have no-one to compare their development to. Other times, it is simply because they're scared of the label and believe there's a stigma attached to a diagnosis of ASC.

Of course, on some occasions, parents are absolutely right to question a diagnosis. There are children diagnosed with ASC where the diagnosis does not seem to fit comfortably. Maybe the parents have tried all the strategies which have been advised for children with ASC and found they don't work. Perhaps their child has only a few of the traits.

Why do children reject a diagnosis?

There are also a lot of children who question their own diagnosis. In my experience, this tends to happen in adolescence, when children become aware of their diagnosis and start to question their own identity and their place in the world. While for some children having a diagnosis can be a comfort and may help them to explain how they view the world, for others it is a label they absolutely do not want.

Is ASC ever misdiagnosed?

Yes, ASC can be misdiagnosed. For a start, the assessment is not perfect. Most parts of the assessment depend on the information that people provide. What people recollect and share can be selective and therefore not always accurate. In addition, some children end up being right on the threshold between a diagnosis of ASC and no diagnosis. It stands to reason, therefore, that sometimes children will receive a diagnosis when perhaps they shouldn't and vice versa.

There are many other diagnoses which have a similar presentation to ASC. Sometimes an ASC diagnosis is initially given when attachment issues, bi-polar disorder, eating disorders or anxiety (to name a few) might be the correct diagnosis.

> What people recollect and share can be selective and therefore not always accurate.

What should I do if my child rejects their diagnosis?

The first thing to do is listen. This might be something that your child has spent a long time thinking about; the least you can do is hear them out. I can't guarantee that the conversation will be an easy one, but it could be a very important one.

Personally, I would explain that a diagnosis of ASC means only as much as they wish it to. If they want everyone to know about it, that's fine. If they want to forget about it and carry on with their life as if it never happened, that is also fine. Explaining that knowing their diagnosis can help them make adaptations to the way they live might also be useful.

If, at the end of the day, they decide their diagnosis is wrong, there are options. Most easily they can simply disregard their diagnosis, tell no-one about it and get on with their life. But for some, this won't be enough. They won't want to think that there is official medical paperwork out there with their name and a diagnosis on it. If this is the case, it is worth seeking a second opinion. The first step in doing this would be to approach your GP or SENCo.

CASE STUDY

Natasha

In the short term, the diagnosis of Asperger syndrome helped. I think it helped Natasha to understand why she was feeling the way she was. I think it helped her to realise that she wasn't the only person in the world who found some social situations confusing and stressful. It was a help to know that not everyone automatically knows what to do in social situations; she wasn't alone. The difference between how she approached life back before the diagnosis and the way she approaches it now is astounding.

But Natasha doesn't like to talk about autism. In fact, on a few occasions she has spoken to us about how she doesn't believe she has ASC. She has also mentioned having her diagnosis changed. We've tried to explain how we feel that the diagnosis has helped her. We've said that she doesn't need to share it with anyone if she doesn't want to and I'd guess that she won't volunteer the information to anyone for a long time, if ever.

Sometimes I wonder why we went for the diagnosis. Sometimes she worries about it. Sometimes she rejects the diagnosis. So we don't talk about it often. She knows how to make adaptations in social situations now, and knows that sometimes she needs to ask for help. And that, as far as I'm concerned, is the most important part. Maybe one day she'll also come round to see that a diagnosis of ASC is a positive thing. Or maybe she'll demand a second opinion.

Reports

They say that two things in life are guaranteed: death and taxes. For those who have a child with ASC, a third certainty can be added – reports. After your child has been seen by a professional (let's say, an educational psychologist or a speech and language therapist (SLT)), the professional will usually write a report on their findings and send a copy to you.

Why are these reports important?

While you may come to dread these reports, they can be very important. Often, the report will come with a host of recommendations for the school setting or home, which aim to help your child. For instance, a report from an SLT might, among other things, recommend that your child takes part in social communication groups which will help develop their reciprocal conversation skills. They would most likely recommend how often this should happen and whether it is something best done in school or clinic. This will be important to the school as it will help them be more specific in the kind of support they offer your child. If the school don't put the recommendations into place, having a copy of the report will help you to hold them to account.

In order to write a report, various assessments are often undertaken with your child which help to pinpoint as accurately as possible where your child's strengths and difficulties are. While sometimes these might simply confirm your suspicions, there are times when results from assessments can prove enlightening and, on occasion, surprising. Once again, the ultimate outcome of this is that both you and the school can be more confident in your understanding of what will help your child.

Beyond this, reports can also help to build up a base of evidence should your child need extra support. If the support and strategies which have been recommended are in place but difficulties still remain, you and the school may decide that extra support is needed. This is most often in the form of an Education, Health and Care Plan (EHCP) (see page 50 for more on EHCPs and how to apply for them).

The power of headed notepaper

The reports which have been written about your child carry with them a lot of power. There is weight behind those words. Because they have been written on headed paper, those in a position to make a difference for your child (schools, social workers, local authorities) will sit up and take notice. Use this to your advantage. It's unlikely you'll ever want to frame the reports or maybe even show them to anyone you know. But they can open doors for you. They can get you respite. They can make sure your child gets a place at the school which can best meet their needs. They can make sure that extra funding is released to help your child succeed. Use them wisely.

Depressing reading

Sometimes these reports can make pretty depressing reading for a parent, though. They're not like the end-of-term school reports you might be used to receiving, which usually focus on the positives and dress up any negatives in fairly euphemistic language (e.g. 'Johnny

> A well-written report should try to focus on what your child can do, as well as what they can't do.

is a lively and energetic boy' instead of 'Johnny spends most of his time running around the classroom and turning tables and chairs over'). In a report from a professional, the language is likely to be more clinical. If Johnny turned tables over and then jumped out of the window during the assessment, that is what the report will say. Sometimes this can make difficult reading. You might read it and think there is no hope for your child, or that the report only focuses on the things your child struggles with.

A well-written report should try to focus on what your child can do, as well as what they can't do. But the reason the report was commissioned and written was to help address the things they have difficulty with. A report which downplays difficulties wouldn't be much use. Therefore, you might be best choosing a time when you're feeling strong to sit down and wade through a new report.

What language is this written in?

As is often the case in SEN, reports can be heavy on jargon, making them nigh on impossible to decode for the layman (you'll find a glossary of acronyms on page 161). While you'll probably soon be fluent in ASC jargon, you might like to ask for support when reading a report to begin with. In most cases, the professional who wrote the report should be able to go through it with you, explaining in plainer terms what it means. If this isn't possible, you might ask the school, a support group or a SEN advocate to help. An internet search can often help to find definitions of some of the terms too.

Hang on, this report isn't accurate...

By and large, what you read in reports is accurate, as it should be. But the reports are written by humans, and humans, as we know, are capable of making mistakes. Therefore, I've read some reports which have mistakenly changed factual information. Very often, I've read reports where sections have been cut and pasted from old reports and still contain the names of other children. Most worryingly of all, I've read one or two reports where drastic changes to provision are recommended (usually discharging from a service) without any evidence or assessment information to back them up. My suspicion is that this is often a way for overstretched services to cut their caseload. The problem is, because they're written on headed notepaper, they carry a huge weight. Once a professional has written something that is not entirely accurate on headed notepaper, it becomes gospel. It might be submitted to a panel making a very important decision about your child. It might be used to write part of your child's EHCP. In the worst-case scenario, it could be used as evidence to remove a service or support from you or your child.

> If you notice something that isn't quite right in a report you receive, it is important to lodge a complaint immediately.

So if you notice something that isn't quite right in a report you receive, it is important to lodge a complaint immediately. If possible, try to speak to the person who wrote the report and ask them to alter and reissue it so that it is correct. This is important for you and your child, but also for the author of the report. They would certainly not wish their mistakes to come to light at a tribunal and would rather put them right at the earliest opportunity. However, if you try this and have no joy getting alterations made, you might like to speak to your local Parent Partnership SEN Support Worker (note that their job title might be slightly different), who will be able to advise you on the best course of action.

Information sharing

When a report is written, you will have a say over who it can be shared with. If you do not wish for some services to receive a copy, it is usually within your power to stop them from obtaining one. The only likely extenuating circumstance would be if there was a safeguarding concern, in which case your wishes could be overridden. However, usually you will want all the professionals in contact with your child to have as much information as they can, and will therefore want the reports to be shared.

Respite

In order to look after a child with ASC (or indeed any child) you need to take care of yourself as well. It is very easy to treat your own wellbeing as something of an afterthought, but making sure that you are happy and healthy will benefit everyone. While this looks simple enough written down, we all know that in the middle of hectic day-to-day life, finding time to look after yourself can be difficult. Sometimes you will need a break from caring, and one way to get this is through respite care.

Respite care

Respite care may form part of your care plan if you are a carer for your child. It can be arranged by the local authority (LA), although there is also scope for you to have a direct payment from your LA so you can arrange care yourself. Respite care can take different forms, dependent on your needs and what suits. For instance, the care can be simply to hire someone to do what you already do, so you can take a break for a while. Alternatively, it could take the form of the person you care for spending a short time in a residential home or day centre, so the whole family can have a break. The care can also take the form

> Making sure that you are happy and healthy will benefit everyone.

of holidays for the carer and the young person with ASC. How regularly these respite breaks happen will vary and will depend upon your parent carer needs assessment. Your LA should be able to give you more information on the options open to you, if you are not sure.

Parent carer needs assessment

A parent carer needs assessment is an assessment made by the LA. The aim is not to make a judgement on your parenting skills, but to look at the whole picture of family life and assess whether extra support or services may be needed. A care plan will be drawn up, which may include some respite care. If you haven't had a parent carer needs assessment, you can contact your LA to arrange one.

Family and friends

If you have a supportive network of family and friends, it may be that you can arrange some respite yourself. It's important to remember that this may put a strain on them, though, in the same way that it can do for you. You may also need to provide family and friends with some background information and support in order for them to be able to give you a break – explaining routines and strategies that work in various situations will help the experience go much more smoothly.

Babysitting

Most parents don't have to think twice about getting a babysitter to look after their children while they have an evening out. But for many parents of children with ASC, getting a babysitter to look after their children seems like an impossible dream. Often, parents of children with ASC are so loath to get a babysitter that they'd prefer to stay in rather than risk coming home to a trashed house or frazzled babysitter. This needn't be the case though. There are babysitting agencies out there who can supply babysitters with experience in ASC and often, with a bit of pre-planning, you'll find that you have friends and family who are both willing and able to help out so you can get out of the house.

Routines (and change)

Humans are creatures of habit. For people with autism, routines and habits are often very important, providing a structure to their day. In a sometimes confusing world, daily routines provide predictability, comfort and reassurance.

Why is routine important?

Establishing a routine can be extremely important. It will help build structure and familiarity to your child's day and that may help them to be less anxious as they will feel they have some control over what is happening to them. When children with ASC start school, which

> In a sometimes confusing world, daily routines provide predictability, comfort and reassurance.

can be a difficult time for them, often the routine is one thing which helps them to cope. In fact, often it is the parts of the day where there are unexpected changes to routine (such as school trips, supply teachers or fire alarms) which will cause difficulty for many children with ASC.

Can it be a problem?

Yes, routine can sometimes become a problem. Let's say, for instance, your child has got into the routine that at dinner time, they eat a bowl of plain pasta and nothing else. When you try to make this meal a little healthier by adding vegetables to it, your child refuses to eat. You have altered their routine and a battle of wills is likely to ensue. Or, for example, your child may have decided that there is only one toilet cubicle at school that they will use. If the cubicle which they visit is suddenly in use, this can become something of a problem.

It can also be problematic if your child is so dependent on a certain routine that they become fearful of it changing. In that case, rather than the routine becoming a way of easing anxiety, it ends up creating more.

It isn't always easy to work out whether a particular routine is a good one to have. To determine this, you may need to analyse the behaviour and determine whether the routine is:

- harming anyone
- helping to minimise anxiety or instead causing anxiety
- interfering with the child's social life
- interfering with family life
- stopping your child learning.

Change

While routine is reassuring to people with ASC, change, transition and unpredictability can be unsettling and a cause of anxiety. Any kind of change, from small things like transitions between activities to larger things like starting a new school, changing classes, moving home or going on holiday, can be difficult. But change is a part of life, and by teaching your child to accept, understand and deal with change, you will be equipping them for life.

How can I help manage change?

With a little planning and preparation, you can help your child to adapt to changes in routine.

- **Talk through what will happen** and what they can do if they are feeling anxious about it. Preparing your child for change will often help them to cope.
- **Use visual aids** (see page 158) such as a visual timetable or a now and next card. These resources visually map out the tasks/ lessons/activities which will be coming up so your child knows what is happening, when, and for how long.
- **Use an oops card.** This is a card to be placed on a visual organiser to show that something in the timetable has changed. I've known an oops card completely change the way a pupil approaches change – from being highly anxious about changes to the timetable, to celebrating when a change came about. I'd recommend that when you introduce an oops card, you manipulate the situation in your favour – engineer a change in the timetable so you can put in something the child will love to do. Do this a few times and often the results are astounding.
- **Use social stories** if there is a particular change coming up which you anticipate your child may struggle with, or a change in routine or transition which has caught your child out on a few occasions. Social stories may also help if there is a certain part of a routine

which your child struggles to understand or cope with (for instance, brushing teeth before bed).

Follow the rules

Children with ASC are often (but not always) sticklers for the rules. Rules provide the ultimate structure for children who actively seek boundaries. This is often a really good thing (let's face it, nobody likes a cheat!) but it can sometimes cause friction when someone else is bending the rules slightly and they seem to be getting away with it.

This can be just as true in general life as in playing games. As parents we usually stick to the rules, but just occasionally there are times when we need to stray from them – this can then end up being an area of anxiety for a child. I've also known situations where children with ASC have desperately wanted to stick to the rules, but there has been one which they've found difficult to manage (for instance, with good listening rules, I've known children who have got upset because they were unable to sit still due to their sensory needs). Therefore, it's worth thinking through any rules you set for your child and agreeing them together before setting them in stone.

S *is for*

School (choosing the right one)

Getting the right school for your child is *really* important, although you probably don't need me to tell you that. It can be complicated and frustrating, but it is entirely doable.

What you'll need

To know your own child

The good news is that the first thing you need is to know your own child. Seeing as you are the world's foremost expert on your child, this should be the easy bit. You know how your child is likely to react in different settings, and this will be vital in finding the right provision for them.

An open mind

You will also need an open mind. There are lots of different options for schooling out there as long as you're willing to consider them. Many people have pre-conceived ideas about schools, whether from listening to other parents, experiences from their own schooling or simply from a hunch. The only way to truly judge a school is by seeing it in action – so get out there and visit as many as you can.

Luck

Next, you'll need a slice of luck. This is another of those postcode lottery situations. In some education authorities you'll be spoilt for choice when choosing a school – you might have a selection of excellent mainstream schools, special schools and units attached to mainstream schools. In others, you may be left scratching your head at the dearth of appropriate schools for your child. If you have your mind set on a specialist provision for your child, you may also need luck in applying at just the right time to get the last space available. A general rule of thumb is to apply as early as you can.

Patience

Of course, you're also going to need loads of patience. Bags and bags of it. First of all, you'll need it to exhaustively explore all the options. But you'll also need patience as you wait for the whole slow process to pass through the many layers of bureaucracy that are almost inevitable in SEN.

Persistence

Add to this a generous helping of persistence. You will need to be fighting your child's corner the whole way. There may be times when you feel you're getting nowhere, but keep communicating with those people who have the power to influence the decision-making process. In my experience, the parents who persist (in a polite way) get way more out of the SEN system than those who don't.

Support

Finally, you'll need support. This could be in the form of a family member or friend, someone who has been through the same process, a teacher or Special Educational Needs Coordinator (SENCo), or local authority (LA) parent adviser or case worker. I'd suggest taking advice and support from each and every one of these people. You could start by asking the LA parent adviser or case worker which schools in the local area might be suitable for your child. Any and all information received will help you make a more informed decision.

Types of school provision

Mainstream schools

Mainstream schools are those that are open to all children regardless of whether they have SEN or not. They follow the mainstream curriculum. Many children with ASC attend mainstream schools and, with support, get on just fine.

> There are lots of different options for schooling out there as long as you're willing to consider them.

Special schools

There are many different types of special school which specialise in different areas of SEN, including moderate learning difficulties; severe learning difficulties; profound learning difficulties; social, emotional and mental health difficulties; and sensory impairment, to name but a few. Some children with ASC might attend a special school, particularly if they have other areas of SEN too. Special schools will have their own criteria for entry and a panel which makes decisions on whether pupils meet these criteria and can be offered a place.

Specialist units/additionally resourced provision

These are units which are attached to a mainstream school. The unit will have a specialism, such as ASC or speech and language. The pupils in the unit are usually able to access as much of life in the mainstream part of the school as they can manage, but will also receive extra support in the base from specialist staff. As with special schools, they will have their own criteria for entry and a panel which makes decisions on whether pupils meet these criteria and can be offered a place.

School offer

Each school should have a section on their website where they outline the support they can offer in school. This is called the school offer, and you should make sure to check it out at each school you're considering.

Your rights as a parent of a child with an Education, Health and Care Plan (EHCP)

If your child has an EHCP, their rights as a child and your rights as a parent are foremost in the decision-making process for school placement. These rights are set out in the SEND Code of Practice (2017). Essentially, if you want mainstream provision for your child, you can opt for that and the LA is duty-bound to try to arrange it for you, taking reasonable steps to make sure that the provision is appropriate. In fact, the Code of Practice sets out some specific steps schools can take to ensure children with autism can be taught in a mainstream school. It is only in exceptional cases where the LA might decide mainstream school is not appropriate if parents have expressed a wish for their child to be in a mainstream school.

However, not all children with ASC will have their needs met most effectively in a mainstream school. Therefore, you may want to explore the options available to you for specialist provision. If you want a particular kind of specialist provision, then you are once again entitled to ask for it and the LA will try to meet your wishes.

So, could I ask them to send my child to Eton?

You could try. My guess is that you wouldn't get very far though! You can ask them to place your child in any maintained nursery or school, non-maintained special school, further education or sixth form college, independent school or independent specialist college. Maintained here means a school that is funded and controlled by an LA, whereas non-maintained means a school controlled directly by the Secretary of State (e.g. academies and free schools). The LA is obliged to try to meet your wishes, but there are a few checks and balances to make sure that the placement is right for you, your child, the school and the taxpayer. Whichever school you choose, the LA will start by consulting with the school. This means they send the EHCP document to the school and ask them whether they can meet your child's needs. The school can come back with a yes or a no. If it is a no, you may need to think again. For

> If your child has an EHCP, their rights as a child and your rights as a parent are foremost in the decision-making process for school placement.

most specialist schools, there will be entry criteria to ensure that your child and the school are a good match. However, even if your child meets the entry criteria, the decision about whether they get a place or not goes to a panel. As places in specialist provision are limited, it is possible that your child might meet the criteria but not get a place.

Another thing the LA will take into account is cost. You may have heard about a specialist provision a hundred miles away that sounds perfect for your child. It may well be perfect. But it may also be prohibitively expensive for the LA to send your child there. They may say no to your choice, and instead try to find a similar provision closer to home and at less cost.

Can the LA force a school to take my child, even when they say no?

Yes, they can, and they fairly frequently do. In my experience, some schools will automatically say they can't take a child with SEN as they can't meet their needs. However, if the parents insist, the LA can name the school anyway. While this might seem like a victory to the parents, I would question whether a school that turns your child down because of their needs is the right place for your child, regardless of what exam results it may get. Will it have the kind of inclusive ethos that you'll be looking for? Of course there are many cases where parents have fought for their child's rights and successfully got a place at a school that turned their child down. But there are also many other parents who pressed ahead with a school who initially turned their child down, only for the placement to break down.

Can I appeal decisions?

Yes, absolutely. LAs don't always get decisions correct. Necessity means that they sometimes have considerations (such as cost) which override other concerns. You are therefore within your rights to go to a tribunal to get the Department for Education to make the final decision.

LAs do not like tribunals. They are costly, time-consuming, stressful and put their decision-making process and paper trail under the microscope. They usually do what they can to avoid them, especially as LAs often lose them. I've known cases where a parent has threatened to go to tribunal, and the LA has suddenly changed or reversed a decision, seemingly to avoid being dragged through the process.

It's also worth noting that tribunals are equally time-consuming and stressful for parents. It can also be extremely costly to parents, even if they win; costs are not always covered by the losing party.

What if my child doesn't have an EHCP?

If your child has ASC but no EHCP, choosing the right school is still vitally important. Obviously. A good place to start is schools' websites, where you can view their SEN offers. This is basically where they set out the types of provision that they can offer in school. If you like the sound of what a school has to say, arrange to have a look around. I'd recommend that when you make arrangements to look at the school, you speak to the school's SENCo. That way you can speak to them about your child and their needs, and the SENCo can explain what they might be able to do in order to meet those needs. I would suggest that from that information, you should be able to make an informed decision about whether the school is suitable or not.

Transition

Even more so than for the general school population, transitions can be an area of difficulty for many children with ASC. Transitioning to a new school therefore takes planning, patience and perseverance. The idea, of course, is to prepare for change and anticipate anything that your child might find difficult about the transition to a new school.

The way you approach the transition will depend on a number of things, including your child's age and understanding, past experience of how your child responds to transitions, the time available and information that you have about the new school. For some children, preparations will need to start at the earliest possible opportunity so they have plenty of time to get used to the idea. For others, particularly those that might spend the intervening time worrying, a shorter lead up to transition will be more appropriate. In most cases, you will want to arrange for your child to have some visits to their new school, and possibly for staff from the new school to come and see them in their current school.

If, as is likely for a child with ASC, you think that your child will need help with the social aspect of transition, this should be arranged with the new school. Depending on your child, you may also like to prepare for the transition by talking through any worries to help get round them (maybe using social stories (see page 136)), looking at timetables and maps of the new school, and looking at pictures of people and places in the new school.

SEND Code of Practice

Or, to give it its full name, Special Educational Needs and Disability Code of Practice: 0 to 25 years (2017).

This is a government document which forms statutory guidance for organisations which support children and young people with special educational needs and/or disabilities. It outlines what should happen in all areas of SEND, from Education, Health and Care Plans (EHCPs) to working with health and social care, from resolving disagreements to getting impartial advice. It contains all the information you might need on what educational settings and local authorities should be doing to help your child and you.

It is a very long document (292 pages) and I would never advocate reading it cover to cover, unless of course you are suffering from insomnia, in which case it should help nicely. I would, however, advise that you dip into it from time to time, especially when you have questions about your rights and SEN. I would, for instance, consult it if you have cause to make a complaint, if you are thinking of applying for an EHCP (see page 50 for more on this topic) or transferring your child from primary to secondary school. It is available online at www.gov.uk and is fairly easy to navigate.

Sensory issues

Sensory differences are common in people with ASC and can affect any of the senses. Often, these differences are quite difficult to pinpoint, but can have a big impact on everyday life. For instance, a child who is highly sensitive to loud noises may find situations like public transport, busy school dinner halls and classrooms very stressful. The differences in the way people with ASC respond to sensory stimulus are often divided into being over-sensitive (hypersensitivity) or under-sensitive (hyposensitivity).

The five senses?

We're taught about our five senses from an early age. People with sensory differences could have difficulties processing information from each or any of these senses.

1 Sight
2 Sound
3 Touch
4 Smell
5 Taste

You may not be aware of two systems in your body which are also sensory:

6 Vestibular, which is to do with balance
7 Proprioception, which is our system for body awareness, telling us where our body is in relation to other things and about what each of our body parts is doing

Senses overloaded

The sensory issue that I see most often in children with ASC in mainstream school is difficulty dealing with the amount of sensory information which the world around them is continually pumping out. Commonly, children feel that the world around them is too busy, that they cannot keep up with the constant input of information which all of their senses need to process. This can become overwhelming to the point where they feel overloaded. At times like this, children often shut down in one way or another – by acting out, becoming withdrawn or using their own strategies to try to deal with too much information.

> **When your child is becoming overwhelmed by their environment, rather than trying valiantly to soldier on with what you're doing, it's best to take them out of that environment.**

Have you tried switching it off and on again?

The go-to piece of advice for IT departments worldwide is also worth thinking about if your child suffers from sensory overload. When your child is becoming overwhelmed by their environment, rather than trying valiantly to soldier on with what you're doing, it's best to take them

out of that environment. Think of it as a way of resetting their system – switching them off and then on again – before they can resume. Moving to a quieter space could work. Giving them a physical break (i.e. time to go and let off some steam) may also work. Another option is to let them do an activity which you know helps calm them down. Once they've had a chance to do this, they may be calm enough to continue with what they were doing before.

What does being over-sensitive look like?

Children who are over-sensitive may become overwhelmed by sensory input and this can make it difficult for them to function.

Sight

- Prefers to focus on detail rather than the whole picture
- Has blurred vision
- Is sensitive to light

Sound

- Unable to cut out sounds
- Able to hear things at a seemingly long distance
- Sounds can become distorted and/or muddled

Touch

- May find touch uncomfortable and dislike/avoid being touched
- Dislikes/avoids having anything on hands or feet (e.g. shoes, socks)
- Has difficulty brushing, combing and washing hair
- May dislike some clothes because of the texture and the way they feel against the skin

Smell

- Dislikes powerful smells (e.g. perfume, shampoo, washing powder) and avoids people that smell of them
- Avoids areas with a strong or distinctive smell (e.g. the kitchen, public toilets)
- Gags/feels sick at certain smells
- Detects/complains about odours others can't smell

Taste

- Finds some foods too strong and prefers a restricted diet of bland food
- Reluctant to try new/different foods
- Avoids social situations involving food

Vestibular

- Suffers from travel sickness
- Finds physical activities like sport difficult
- Doesn't like feet being off the ground or head not upright

Proprioception

- Holds themselves in a stiff way and moves whole body to look at something
- Has difficulty with fine motor skills (e.g. doing up buttons and laces, writing, cutting, sewing)
- Appears to be uncoordinated
- Often seems tired

You haven't mentioned being under-sensitive...

Children who are under-sensitive may show this through sensory seeking behaviours.

Sight

- Has poor depth perception, so may appear clumsy and unable to catch and throw etc
- Misses details in their environment
- Loses their place when reading/writing
- May be clumsy and bump into things

Sound

- Enjoys being in extremely noisy places
- Switches off/daydreams
- Does not respond when others are speaking to them
- Likes to make noise (e.g. by humming to themselves)

Touch

- Chews anything and everything
- Likes the feel of heavy items on them (e.g. a weighted backpack or blanket)
- Self-harms
- Smears faeces

Smell

- Tolerates or seems not to notice smelly environments others find offensive (e.g. toilets)
- May have bodily odour without even realising
- Craves foods with strong smells

Taste

- Craves foods with strong flavours
- Craves unusual substances with no nutritional value (e.g. chalk, wood)
- Mouths objects
- Can become obese as a result of trying to meet their own taste needs

Vestibular

- Seeks movement (e.g. by rocking on their chair)
- Enjoys spinning round and doesn't seem to get dizzy
- Appears restless, always on the go
- Seems to be a thrill-seeker and may not understand/see dangers

Proprioception

- Walks on tiptoes or stomps instead of walks
- Presses too hard with a pencil
- Likes to be in small spaces and may invade others' space by standing too close
- Has poor hand–eye coordination

But my child doesn't have sensory issues

It's absolutely true – your child might not have any sensory differences or difficulties. But in my experience with ASC, it is always worth bearing sensory issues in mind. It's also worth noting that sensory difficulties aren't always obvious. Children with ASC won't always tell you when they are struggling to process the sensory information they're being bombarded with – or at least, they usually won't do so in words. What you're more likely to see is a behavioural response. Different children will do this in different ways; one child might start to hum, one might hide under a table, one might trash the room they're in, one might just withdraw into themselves. But if you're seeing these behaviours and can't figure out the trigger for them, it might be worth considering that there could be a sensory processing issue.

> Children with ASC won't always tell you when they are struggling to process the sensory information they're being bombarded with.

Where can I get help?

The first thing to do is to try to work out precisely what your child's sensory needs might be. In some cases, this might be fairly obvious (e.g. if your child covers their ears when they're in loud places). But in many cases, the sensory issues can be hidden. Either way, it is worth speaking to your GP about getting a referral to an occupational therapist. An occupational therapist trained in sensory integration will be able to do an assessment to see exactly where your child has sensory difficulties or differences. One thing to bear in mind, though, is that occupational therapy (OT) is another of those services which can be difficult to come by.

However, if you do manage to get an OT appointment, it's likely that the occupational therapist will do an assessment and provide you with a report and some suggestions for how to help your child. If your child is at school, the assessment is also usually shared with the school as they will be able to implement many of the strategies to help your child. It is less likely that your child will receive ongoing OT input. Most OT services don't have the capacity to do ongoing work with the vast majority of children who are referred to them. However, if you feel your child needs ongoing OT support (a rule of thumb here would be that they might need ongoing support if their sensory differences impair their day-to-day functioning) and has an Education, Health and Care Plan (EHCP), it is worth trying to get some OT provision written into the EHCP. A good way to approach this would be to speak to the Special Educational Needs Coordinator (SENCo) at your child's school or an independent Parent Partnership SEN Support Worker (note that their job title might be slightly different) in the local authority.

George

George paid very little attention in lessons. We tried all manner of behavioural strategies (such as reward charts, reminders of listening behaviour and so on) before we realised the root cause of the problem: George had extremely good hearing but couldn't tune out distractions. This meant that while he was supposed to be listening to me and his classmates, George could hear the bees buzzing outside the window, the air conditioning unit in the IT room next door, people fastening and unfastening the Velcro® on their shoes and even noise from the road, which was right on the other side of the school. He was unable to tune out the sounds he didn't want or need to hear, so the whole mix of sounds was overwhelming. Plus, he was a big fan of transport systems and could tell from the sound of the engine which bus was passing by the front of the school. So, was he more interested in hearing the teacher or the buses? Yeah, you've guessed it – the buses won. And when the sounds were overwhelming him, he would begin to flap his hands.

When we realised that this was the problem, we began to put steps in place to help us make sure that George had a quieter and less busy environment to learn in. We also made sure that we read the signs of when he was feeling overwhelmed by the sensory input of his environment and gave him activities and a space to calm himself down, ready to learn again.

Practical strategies

Anticipating sensory issues and putting steps in place to prevent them becoming a problem is more desirable than allowing your child to get to the point where they're overloaded and anxious. Here are a few things that might help to do that.

Sight

Over-sensitive

- Have a quiet and calm place where the child can go if they are over-stimulated by visual information (a pop-up tent can work well).

- Reduce visual clutter.
- Seat the child away from visual distractions (such as a window).
- Try using a tinted reading ruler and presenting information on coloured sheets rather than white paper.

Under-sensitive

- Create a focal point for the child (e.g. a brightly coloured poster with key information).
- Use a reading ruler to help the child track when reading.
- Use paper with heavy/coloured lines to help the child organise their writing.
- Help the child with visual discrimination skills (e.g. play 'odd one out' games and puzzles).

Sound

Over-sensitive

- Prepare the child if you are going somewhere noisy (e.g. by using a social story or giving the child coping strategies for when they will need them).
- Provide headphones or earplugs to block out unnecessary noises.
- Switch off background noise (such as the radio or television, the washing machine, the vacuum cleaner) and close windows and doors to block out sound.

Under-sensitive

- Visual supports may help.
- Use changes of tone of voice and volume to gain/maintain attention.
- Play listening games (e.g. What's that sound?, Simon says).

Touch

Over-sensitive

- Warn the child before you're going to touch them.
- Allow the child to do tasks such as brushing their hair themselves – this way they can judge how hard to pull the brush.
- Turn clothes inside out so the seam is not touching the child, or alternatively you can find clothes with no seam (there are sensory-friendly suppliers online, and a lot of sports clothing is seamless).
- Change the texture of foods which the child doesn't like the texture of (e.g. by pureeing).

Under-sensitive

- Make sure you monitor the child in situations where they could hurt themselves without realising (e.g. using a hairdryer, touching hot radiators).
- Try deep pressure activities such as heavy weights, press-ups or deep tissue massage.
- Provide alternatives to potentially harmful activities (e.g. chew toys for mouthing, a hot water bottle for feeling heat).
- Encourage handwriting on surfaces which will give tactile feedback (e.g. sandpaper).

Smell

Over-sensitive

- Switch to unscented brands of washing powders, soaps, shampoos etc.
- Encourage the child to take round a container with a smell which they find pleasant inside.
- Try to gradually increase the range of foods they can tolerate.
- Problem-solve and plan with your child where they will go to the toilet when in public places (e.g. the disabled toilet in school).

Under-sensitive

- If bodily odour is a problem, you may wish to choose strong-smelling detergents or perfumes/deodorants.
- Provide food choices which will be healthy (most people without a sense of smell can still taste salty, sweet, sour and bitter flavours so they may seek these out).
- Develop routines around personal hygiene (a social story may be appropriate).
- Play games to help the child identify smells (e.g. What's that smell?).

Taste

Over- sensitive

- Gradually introduce new foods and flavours to the child.
- Give the child information about the food groups and having a healthy, balanced diet.
- Use reward systems for trying new foods.

Under-sensitive

- Give the child the opportunity to supplement their food with strong flavours (e.g. chilli sauce).
- Include a variety of textures in food.
- If the child's attention is starting to flag, allow them something with a strong flavour (e.g. a strong mint).
- Provide a choice of foods, and try to ensure that the child is still able to eat a balanced diet.

Vestibular

Over-sensitive

- Give the child lots of support and practice with physical activities (e.g. going to the park, running, cycling).
- Give your child lots of space when they are practising movements.
- Avoid escalators and lifts where possible and provide support when the child must use them.

Under-sensitive

- Cut down physical activities into smaller steps.
- Incorporate chances to spin/rock/move into the child's routine.
- Let the child sit on a wobble cushion.

Proprioception

Over-sensitive

- Massage the child's joints and limbs to soothe them.
- Use a weighted jacket or blanket to calm them.
- Include movement breaks during the day.

Under-sensitive

- Use a weighted blanket or wobble cushion to provide feedback.
- Include movement breaks during the day.
- Use light-up pens to help the child know how much pressure to exert when writing.
- Encourage deep pressure activities such as seat push-ups and wall press-ups when the child is restless.

Synaesthesia

You may also have heard of synaesthesia, which some people on the autism spectrum have, though it is not exclusive to those with ASC. This is where people take sensory information in through one sense, but experience it through another. For instance, some people hear sounds and see them as colours. Most people with synaesthesia experience it as normal and it has no detrimental effect on their lives. Some, however, have reported suffering sensory overload as a result of synaesthesia.

Siblings

Okay, no beating about the bush here: having a child with ASC can put a strain on family life. And while a lot of support may go the way of the child with ASC or to their parents, siblings can also have a lot to deal with, yet sometimes they go unconsidered.

Before I continue, though, I should add that the impact of having a sibling with ASC will depend on many factors, not least the behaviour of the child with ASC. Often, a child with ASC will present with lots of challenging behaviours at home, but not always. The support network you have around the family may also have an enormous bearing on the impact on siblings.

It's not fair!

Firstly, siblings of children with ASC often feel that home life is unfair. It seems like there's one set of rules for them and another for their sibling with ASC. While this may be necessary to having a peaceful home life, it won't go unnoticed by siblings, whether they choose to loudly remind you of it every five minutes or keep it bottled up inside.

Siblings inevitably also tend to bear the brunt of behaviours. They might be the person on the receiving end of a punch or a kick or a tirade of abuse. They may also find that their sibling with ASC doesn't take their thoughts or feelings into account in their actions and words, which can be confusing and upsetting.

> A lot of support may go the way of the child with the ASC or to their parents, but siblings can also have a lot to deal with.

Out of necessity, the child with ASC can often be the centre of attention. Plans are always built around their interests and needs. They may also demand a lot more of their parents' time.

It's also worth bearing in mind that siblings may not just bear the brunt at home but can also sometimes be the focus of unwanted attention at school, where they can be teased because their brother or sister has a disability or seems different. Obviously this is not always the case as ASC is a hidden disability, but it can happen.

Therefore, it should be no surprise that siblings of children with ASC can feel angry, upset, jealous, sidelined and confused.

How can you help siblings to deal with these feelings?

Plan for special time with siblings

Because their behaviour may be easier to handle and demand less attention, siblings often end up being sidelined. This doesn't mean they actually need less attention though. Try to plan time based around their interests.

Explain ASC to them

This will obviously depend on the age and understanding of your child(ren), but it is important that they understand ASC as much as possible. It will help them appreciate the difficulties their brother or sister has and could enable them to help out in some ways (e.g. by not rising to antagonistic things the sibling with ASC may say). You'll be able to explain why some things their sibling does go unchallenged. It will also help explain why their sibling with ASC has a lack of empathy, if this is the case. There are some excellent pages on the National Autistic Society website which deal with this topic.

Help them stay calm

Siblings of children with ASC will undoubtedly end up at the sharp end of flash points. If you can help them to understand that a calm reaction is the best way to deal with these situations, you'll be doing everyone a favour.

Time alone

Try to help them understand that their brother or sister sometimes needs time alone, how to spot when this is, and encourage them to try to let them be alone when needed.

Support

There are schemes around the country, such as Young Carers (run by The Children's Society), which recognise the role that siblings play in caring for family members with ASC (and lots of other conditions) and give them practical and emotional support, as well as respite in the form of opportunities for days out and activities. They also assess the extent of the care the child is undertaking and whether this is appropriate or not. You may also find that local SEN organisations arrange events and activities specifically for siblings of children with ASC.

Family and friends

If you're lucky enough to have an extended (and helpful) network of family or friends, try to use them. They may be able to spend time with either your child with ASC or their siblings, to allow you and them to have some respite.

A negative experience

Having a sibling with ASC can have a negative impact in many ways. Children can end up doing more care-type tasks to help out in the family. They can end up missing out on some aspects of being a child and be forced to grow up before their time. They can feel scared and resentful. The support they receive will greatly determine the impact having a sibling with ASC has on them.

Conversely, however, helping to care for a sibling with ASC can be a positive experience and one that teaches tolerance, understanding and the value of caring for others.

CASE STUDY

Anthony

My older brother had ASC, though it wasn't diagnosed until he was in his twenties. His condition had all-consuming effects on family life, affecting decisions about where to go on holiday, what to do at the weekend, which schools to go to. Decisions were made around whether it might affect some obsession or plan of my brother; similarly, his obsessions often controlled the way we had to act. It affected me very deeply and in ways I still don't fully understand.

My parents were very supportive of me in terms of their love and attention, but the focus was always on my brother. If, say, my friends wanted to come round, my brother might start screaming until my parents would cave in to him and the visit would be cancelled. At one point I even gave up seeing my friends. It was very isolating.

I received no support, and neither did my parents. They were told that my brother would 'grow out of it' – such nonsense. Fortunately, now he has been diagnosed he lives in sheltered accommodation and has a happy life, but I wish it had happened earlier.

I have often thought throughout my life that there should be some system for the siblings of those with ASC, even if it's just somwhere to talk about it. As a teenager I had some quite severe psychological difficulties which were a direct result of the effects my brother had on home life, but they were brushed aside.

Sleep

Sleep. Blissful, restorative sleep. A refuge from the hectic world around us.

Except, of course, for many children with ASC, sleep is not quite so straightforward. It can take a long time to get to sleep and there may be many awakenings during the night. And, as all parents know from bitter experience, if your child doesn't sleep, neither do you. Fear not, however, for there are ways you can help your child (and yourself) to get a good night's sleep.

Why won't they sleep?!

There can be many different reasons why someone doesn't sleep. Some of these are environmental factors – routines and sensory factors such as light and sound. As many children with ASC also have sensory differences, this may be an important factor in their sleeping habits. There are also neurological, behavioural and medical reasons why sleep may be interrupted.

> Get as clear an idea as you can of what factors might be affecting sleep beforehand – are they environmental, behavioural, neurological or medical?

Many of these factors are more common in the ASC population than in the general population. For instance, children who show hyperactivity (a symptom of ADHD, a condition that commonly co-exists with ASC) find it difficult to switch off at bedtime, seeming to be constantly on the go until finally their batteries run out and they grab a couple of hours' shut-eye. Another factor which may affect sleep is anxiety, which is a common symptom for children with ASC. Other co-existing conditions, such as epilepsy, can interrupt sleep too. It is also thought that some children with ASC don't release the hormone melatonin (the hormone which helps regulate sleep) at the right times of day.

What is lack of sleep doing to my child?

As parents, I'm sure we all know what happens when we don't sleep well – the next day is a struggle. Prolonged lack of sleep can make it more difficult to function, to react appropriately to problems, to make good decisions, to concentrate on the job at hand. Sleep plays an important role in brain development and overall health. Therefore, a lack of sleep impacts our cognition (ability to think), mood, behaviour and health. Improving our sleeping habits can therefore have a positive impact in many ways.

What can I do to help my child get a good night's sleep?

This is what you *really* want to know. Whilst you might want to try a range of different approaches to get your child sleeping, it's a good idea to get as clear an idea as you can of what factors might be affecting sleep beforehand – are they environmental, behavioural, neurological or medical? Having an answer to that question will help you find the right strategies for your child.

In the meantime, here are some suggestions to help your child get a better sleep:

- Make sure your child's room is **dark, quiet and cool**.
- Check that you have thought about your child's **sensory needs** (e.g. can your child hear the television from their room? Are their pyjamas made from a material which they like the feel of?).
- Make the **bedtime routine** predictable and include **calming activities** such as a bath, reading a story or listening to quiet music.
- Try to **avoid using screens** (phones, computers, TVs, tablets etc) close to bedtime.
- Help your child to get their **body clock** regular – try to make sure their weekend sleep routine is similar to that during the week.
- **Avoid caffeine**, especially close to bedtime.
- Encourage your child to **exercise** during the day. This can help children to get a deeper sleep.
- Teach your child to **fall asleep on their own**. Many young children become reliant on having a parent close to them to fall asleep. This will be especially helpful if they wake in the night, as they can get themselves back to sleep rather than needing an adult to come into the room to help them.
- If your child is on medication, **check side effects** to see if one may be disturbed sleep. If this is the case, a medical professional may be able to help you by altering the dose, changing the medication, or advising a different time for your child to take the medication to help them get a better sleep.
- If your child suffers from anxiety, give them strategies to **stop thinking about their worries** at bedtime. For instance, worry dolls could help your child to let go of anxieties.
- If you feel like you've tried everything and your child's sleep is still an issue, seek a referral to a **sleep specialist**.
- Some children with persistent insomnia may need **medication** prescribing or **behavioural therapy** to help them sleep.

Social stories

If you haven't yet heard of social stories, this section may change your life.

Social stories are one of the easiest and most useful strategies to use with children with ASC. The simple idea behind them is that they teach children how to deal with a social situation which they are finding problematic. They were created by Carol Gray in 1991 and have been helping people with ASC ever since.

Why use a social story?

People with ASC often find it difficult to understand social situations and how to react in them. As a result, all sorts of undesirable or inappropriate behaviours can crop up. In addition, not knowing what to do in social situations is a big cause of anxiety. Social stories are

> Social stories teach children how to deal with a social situation which they are finding problematic.

designed to help explain the situation and what to do when it next arises. For example, if a child has difficulty sharing, a social story can help to explain why we share and how to do it.

Do they work?

Very simply, yes, most of the time social stories work. Sometimes they work perfectly first time. Other times they're used in conjunction with other strategies and begin to work their magic over a longer timeframe. Occasionally, a social story won't work and you'll need to go back to the drawing board. There are a number of factors which can dictate how successful your story is.

The child

The first and most important factor is who the social story is for. In my experience, some children are more responsive to social stories than others. Those who have more social insight and a desire to understand and conquer a social difficulty tend to respond best because they're actively invested in the process. In these cases, they've been frustrated by a problem they can't seem to figure out and welcome the guidance a social story offers them. They tend to put suggestions into practice right away and success can be instant (depending on the nature of the problem they were experiencing). Developing the social story with the child is a good way to make sure that they are invested in the process.

The situation

Another factor which will affect how well the story works is the situation itself. Some situations are easier to problem-solve than others. For example, I made a video social story with a boy who had difficulty finding things to do at playtime and lunchtimes and felt lonely. There were a couple of suggestions to help him, among which were some clubs he could go to at lunchtimes. Within minutes of sharing the social story, he had taken the advice on board and had taken himself to the playtime club mentioned in the story. Success! I think the main reason this was so successful was because the action the boy needed to do to solve his initial problem was relatively straightforward. On occasions when the action needed to solve the problem is more complex (e.g. staying calm when things don't go your way), I've found social stories have been less successful or slower to have the desired effect.

Quality

The quality of the social story itself is also a factor. A social story needs to be clear in describing the problem and the solution. You'll need to know the level of understanding of the child you're writing for (or with) to assess whether your story does this. What's more, the solution needs to be achievable. Sometimes social stories fall down because of the way they're written. However, a little editing can usually make them more successful.

Where can I find them?

You can find social stories on most subjects with a quick internet search. There are also many books out there with examples of social stories (including my own *Otis the Robot* series, available from www.ldalearning.com). Bear in mind though that any social story you find in a book or on the internet will either have been written fairly generically, or will have been written specifically to meet the needs of another child. Either way, you'll need to adapt the story to meet the needs of the child you are working with.

Can I write one myself?

Anyone can create a social story, provided that a) they can write and b) they can problem-solve the situation which needs explaining and solving. Here's a quick guide to how to do it:

1) Identify the behaviour/situation and the goal

Start by identifying the problematic behaviour or situation. Sometimes the problem will jump out at you, but other times you may need to do a little detective work. You may see the child's behaviour (e.g. hitting another pupil) but what you need to uncover is the trigger for the behaviour. You'll also need to think of what you want the young person to achieve by the time they've used the story. When you have this information, you're ready to go.

2) Give it a title

The title should reflect exactly what the story is about. Quite often it is a good idea to start with *How to...* or to phrase the title as a question.

What can I do if I am stuck on my work?

3) Add descriptive sentences

Start your social story with a few short, simple sentences establishing the facts of the situation. So that the story is focused on the child, write in the first person.

In class we do lots of work. Sometimes I am able to do it on my own. Other times I find my work difficult or don't understand what to do. When I don't understand my work or find it difficult, I get worried.

4) Add affirmative sentences

These are positive sentences which are added to affirm the previous sentence.

This is okay.

5) Add control sentences

These can be added to provide personal meaning and context.

Completing my work is important as it shows the teacher I have understood the lesson.

6) Add directive sentences

Next, add some directive sentences. These gently explain what to do if the situation described occurs.

If I don't know what to do, I should ask an adult. I can raise my hand and wait for them to come to me.

7) Add co-operative sentences

Co-operative sentences show how someone else can help in the situation.

The adult will help me to understand my work.

8) Add some pictures

Depending on the young person you're working with and their understanding of language, you may want to add pictures which help to illustrate the story. Alternatively, you might wish to add pictures of a favourite character to make the story more appealing.

I would always recommend working on the story with the young person for whom the story is intended to make sure that the story addresses the problem as they see it and that the suggested solution is something they think they'll be able to do.

Do they have to be on paper?

Not necessarily. Most social stories will be written on paper, but this isn't the only way to communicate one. What's more, for many children, this may not be the best way to learn what to do in a social situation. Using other forms of communication, such as video clips, may prove more engaging and successful for some children than writing the social story on paper.

CASE STUDY

Mohamed

A little while ago, I was working with a child, Mohamed, who found a whole host of social situations confusing and stressful. I figured that the best thing to do was to write some social stories.

However, every time one of the social stories was brought out, Mohamed would refuse point blank to read it. To begin with I was frustrated, wondering how we could get around the problem. And then I realised that all I needed to do was tune into his interests. He loved using computers and tablets. So the next time we needed a social story, I told Mohamed that we were going to work together to film it. We worked together to problem-solve the social situation which was causing difficulty and then filmed the social story (and narrated and edited it) together. Instantly, his attitude to social stories was changed and he couldn't wait to watch and share what he'd done. What's more, we also managed to key into his interests and Mohamed got to develop some computing skills for a particular purpose.

Special Educational Needs Coordinator (SENCo)

There is a SENCo in every school. Sometimes they get called other things (such as inclusion manager or Special Educational Needs and Disabilities Coordinator (SENDCo)) but they all have fundamentally the same job: to ensure that all learners who need extra support get it. And for that reason I advise all parents of children with either suspected or diagnosed ASC to make a beeline for the school's SENCo. (As I mentioned earlier, I am a SENCo at a primary school in south London, and have been for over ten years.)

Make them your friend. They have experience and expertise in working with children with ASC. They should also know how the education and healthcare systems work, which could save you a lot of headaches and heartache. Please also bear in mind that SENCos may have multiple roles in a school (e.g. class teacher, deputy or assistant head, PE coordinator) so they are often extremely busy people. It is also fairly common for schools (especially smaller primaries) to have a part-time SENCo.

Most children with ASC (but not all) will probably require some kind of support in order to achieve well and be happy in school. The SENCo, working together with you and the class teacher, will be the person that makes sure this happens. They'll also be the person to speak to if you're seeking a referral for an assessment of ASC for your child. They should be able to talk you through the symptoms you're seeing at home and those that are seen in school, and refer you if necessary.

It's fairly common for children with ASC to need other services to help get their provision in school right. The SENCo is the key person in making sure this happens. They can make sure that your child gets the right access to speech and language therapists, autism specialists, educational psychologists and occupational therapists. I should, though, add a qualifying statement here: they can get you access to the right professionals, presuming that those professionals exist in your local area and you meet the referral criteria. If they/you don't, the SENCo should be able to advise you on why not and what to do next.

In many cases, it may be necessary for a child with ASC to have an Education, Health and Care Plan (EHCP). This is a legal document which brings with it extra funding and a long-term plan for your child's education. The SENCo will be the person who speaks to you about EHCPs and how the process of getting one works. If you are all in agreement that an EHCP would be beneficial, the SENCo will get the ball rolling by filling in and sending off the application paperwork. They'll also be responsible for making sure the provision recommended in the EHCP is put in place. They'll hold an annual review meeting each year to make sure things are on track (see page 6).

It will probably also be the SENCo who helps you to sort out changes in school provision (e.g. moving from primary to secondary school, or changing from mainstream to specialist provision). This will certainly be the case if your child has an EHCP, but would also be advisable if they don't.

Of course, as with anything, there are good SENCos and there are less-than-good SENCos. If you find that your school's is the latter, you may like to look elsewhere for guidance. In that case, I'd recommend searching out the Parent Partnership SEN Support Worker at your local authority – they may have a different job title, but should exist – or a local support group.

It's also worth remembering that sometimes the SENCo's job will entail telling you things that you don't want to hear. Sometimes it might be because the health and education systems can be frustrating places and they haven't managed to secure you the result you want. Other times it could be because they're advising you to look at other provision. They will be trying to do what's best for you and your child in a less-than-perfect system – don't shoot the messenger.

School offer

Each school should have their own offer which is available to view on their website. Essentially, this is a rundown of what they can offer in terms of SEN support. This is worth checking out before you choose a school. It is also something worth checking to make sure that the offer matches what your child is getting in school. The SENCo will be responsible for writing and implementing the school offer, so if you have any questions about it, speak to them.

SEND Code of Practice (2017)

Everything that happens in schools around SEN is governed by the Code of Practice (see page 119). This is a document produced by the government which outlines the guidelines for SEN practice. Schools (and therefore SENCos) should be adhering to it in their practice. If they aren't, you have grounds for a complaint. To make a complaint, in the first place you should speak to the SENCo and see if they can resolve it. If this doesn't work, you should follow the school's complaint procedure (details of which should be on their website). If the complaint is still not satisfactorily resolved, you should complain to your LA.

Special interests

Special interests are essentially just hobbies, although they're marked out by how highly focused and obsessional they can become. A special interest can be anything – buses, trains, underground trains, computer games, timetables, dinosaurs, other people, music, art, football clubs... the list is endless. If something exists (come to think of it, even if it doesn't exist), it will be someone's special interest.

Can special interests be beneficial?

The simple answer is yes. The order, routine and repetitiveness that special interests can offer are often reassuring to people with ASC. When the world becomes too overwhelming, special interests can provide a coping mechanism. For many people with autism, their special interests are vital to their wellbeing. As well as providing a place of sanctuary, special interests help to provide a social life and a way to start a conversation with others who share the interest.

Do I need to stop my child from becoming obsessed with something?

No. A special interest or even an obsession is mostly a good thing. I would say, for the most part, that they should be encouraged. In fact, there are many ways that you can harness a special interest which can help make a positive difference in other areas of someone's life:

> When the world becomes too overwhelming, special interests can provide a coping mechanism.

Social life

It may be appropriate to help someone with ASC join a club based around their interest, where they will be able to meet and socialise with people with a common interest.

Conversation

As many people with ASC have difficulty initiating and maintaining conversation, it can be helpful to show them how to use their knowledge of their special interest to start conversations. However, you may also find the opposite – your child may never stop talking about their special interest and may not pick up on non-verbal signals that show when the listener is bored!

Future

Encouraging the hobby/interest/obsession can sometimes prove worthwhile for the future. For example, an interest in subjects such as computers, history, sports or music when they're younger can be valuable when they come to do those subjects at school, or even when they're considering potential careers.

Quality time

Sharing (or at least pretending to share) their special interest can help you to spend some quality time with your child.

Learning

Use the child's interest to help them learn. Not only can they learn more about their special interest, it can often be harnessed to help them in other areas. As homework is often an area of conflict for families (especially those with a child with ASC), making an arrangement with school that homework assignments can be based around areas of interest to the child can be an excellent way of easing the stress and getting a much higher quality of finished product.

Can special interests be a problem?

In general, special interests are a good thing. However, there can be a point at which they become problematic. If the person seems unable to stop obsessional behaviour around their interest, or if they seem upset or distressed while doing it, it could be a sign that the special interest is becoming a problem. Likewise if the interest is limiting their social opportunities or causing disruption to their life (or others' lives). In some cases, the special interest could be something which is inappropriate or undesirable. If this is the case, you may need to think about how you can help them make a change.

How can I help if the interest becomes a problem?

In order to help, you'll need to undertake some detective work. To start, you'll need to think about what the function of the interest or associated behaviour is. Is it to soothe? To deal with anxiety? To block a noise? To negotiate a way out of a stressful social situation?

Once you have this information, you can start to put in place strategies to help. Social stories might be useful to help explain the problem and what can be done instead. One strategy could be to set boundaries (e.g. the amount of time they spend on the computer), or to specify a time of day that is set aside for the hobby or interest.

In some cases, you might be hoping to replace an interest entirely and this can be tricky, especially if the behaviour or interest has been going on for a long time. Again, it might be a good idea to set boundaries. Over time, you may be able to replace the original interest with something more appropriate. For instance, someone who is not old enough to play a violent computer game but who becomes obsessed with it could be guided towards a more appropriate game. Of course, this is likely to cause anxiety for the person with ASC, so make sure that you plan for ways to help ease this anxiety, such as providing other relaxing activities like stress balls, calming music etc.

Speech and language therapy (SALT)

SALT. No, not the kind you put on your chips. Speech and language therapy.

Speech and language therapists (SLTs) are often key professionals for children with ASC. If you think about the triad of impairments (see page 155) – social communication, social interaction and social imagination – it is all about how we communicate with others. For that reason, many children with ASC will have some input from SALT.

Within the autism spectrum, though, there is a wide range of speech and language needs. Some children will have excellent speech and understanding, but might need a helping hand with solving problems with social situations. On the other hand, some may be non-verbal and require intense support to help them communicate through symbols, gestures and signs.

> SLTs are often key professionals for children with ASC: the triad of impairments is all about how we communicate with others.

What can SALT do for my child?

The simple answer is *loads*. Here are some of the ways it may be able to help.

Social communication

Social communication is one area of the triad of impairments. While we convey a lot of meaning in what we say, we often convey just as much in the way we say it through tone of voice, context, sarcasm, non-literal language, body language and facial expressions. This comes naturally to most people, but for those with ASC it can be a big challenge and often the source of misunderstanding and conflict. SALT concentrates on teaching these skills explicitly so children are more equipped to understand not just what is said, but what is *meant.*

Social interaction

Social interaction deals with areas such as understanding social rules, making and maintaining friendships, eye contact and understanding the behaviour of other people. This is another area of the triad of impairments which can cause problems for those with ASC. SALT will help children develop the skills needed to better understand and cope in social situations. Strategies SLTs might suggest could range from roleplay and group work, to social stories and comic strip conversations (see pages 136 and 30) which will help reduce anxiety.

Social imagination

This is the third area in the triad of impairments, which can include difficulties with imaginative play, struggling to predict events and behaviour, difficulty dealing with new or different situations and understanding the emotions and feelings of others (and self). SALT can help equip children with the strategies to cope with change and new or unexpected situations.

Receptive and expressive language

Many children with ASC have delays with either their receptive language (understanding what is said to them) or expressive language (thinking of what they want to say and/or saying it), or both. SLTs have a toolkit of assessments at their disposal to be able to identify specifically where a child's strengths and difficulties lie. Once these have been identified, they can then be very specific in setting targets and arranging provision to help the child with their understanding of language.

Active listening skills

There are occasions for us all when we don't quite hear, process or understand what is said to us. For those with a language delay, this happens much more frequently. While most of us would simply ask for clarification or repetition, many children with ASC and a language delay do not. However, with some training, children can become better at active listening. Teaching the skills of asking someone to repeat, clarify or speak more slowly or clearly can help them to get a lot more from conversations and make a big difference to their ability to access the language in lessons at school. SLTs can help children develop active listening strategies to help them take greater ownership of their understanding of language.

How do I get my child referred?

If you are concerned about your child's speech and language, you can speak to either your GP or health visitor and they can make a referral to SALT. It is also possible for schools to refer, and you could speak to your child's class teacher or Special Educational Needs Coordinator (SENCo) about this. Alternatively, you could make the referral yourself.

However, this is another area where the postcode lottery may be in operation. The criteria and age range will be different depending on where you live. (For instance, until recently in my local authority (LA), it wasn't possible to make new referrals for children over the age of five to be seen by the NHS SALT service.) However, if you speak to your GP, they should be able to advise you on the cut-off age for new referrals and any other criteria the referral would have to meet.

What if my child is too old to be referred?

If you don't meet the criteria based purely on age, there are other options. There are a lot of independent companies and self-employed SLTs out there who are more than willing to take on new children, regardless of their age. The downside to this is that it will cost you money. You may be able to convince the school or LA that they should pay for it, but don't hold your breath.

If your child has an Education, Health and Care Plan (EHCP), a package of SALT will often form a key part of your child's plan and provision. This support does not rely on your child having to be a certain age as the need has already been identified.

If you don't have an EHCP and you can't afford to shell out for private SALT, it might be worth speaking to the SENCo at your child's school about whether they can buy in any SALT advice or ongoing provision, or arrange for school staff members to support your child.

Stimming

Stimming is what most people in the ASC community say instead of the medical term 'self-stimulating behaviour', which is a bit of a mouthful. Stimming tends to be a repetitive movement or sound of some kind (e.g. rocking, making hand movements, flapping, feeling textures, squealing, head banging). It isn't just people with ASC who stim; many people with other developmental disorders, as well as many neurotypical people, stim too.

CASE STUDY

Tom

When it came to playing, I thought I was the expert. I've always loved playing with kids and had masses of energy for it. So it was baffling to me that I couldn't get anything out of my youngest, Tom. Tom's communication delay became more pronounced and alongside the fact that his socialising and play was so limited, it became obvious that an ASC diagnosis was inevitable. Tom had also had hearing problems for over a year and this further hampered his development. I decided that if I wanted to help him, I was going to need to employ some of the strategies that speech and language therapists use.

I now have a collection of games and strategies that occupy Tom, some of which are for the development of speech. Here are two strategies that have been of great value to me. Firstly, I now make sure I always give Tom choices. I never just automatically give him what he wants, but instead expect him to verbalise it. We started at a one-word level ('Chocolate or hairbrush?'). We then moved on to two words ('Tom's chocolate or Mummy's chocolate?') and then three words ('Tom eat chocolate or Tom hide chocolate?').

Secondly, I use automatic speech with Tom, which I learnt from a resource called *Teach Me To Talk* (www.teachmetotalk.com). The idea with automatic speech is using a small amount of language repetitively so that it becomes automatic. A great example is 'Ready, Steady, Go!' It also works really well with nursery rhymes and repetitive books. The adult teaches the repetitive phrase and then eventually says part of the phrase, leaving a pause for the child to fill (i.e. 'Ready, Steady...'). This is one of the few ways I can get Tom to verbalise.

Why stim?

For the most part, people stim because it feels good. Mostly, they stim when they are anxious or overexcited. This includes when the sensory environment becomes overwhelming (e.g. too noisy or busy). (See page 119 for more on sensory issues.) The repetitive movement of stimming can help people to feel calmer by blocking out the stressful sensory environment, which can help them to rebalance and refocus. Many neurotypical people also stim in stressful situations. For instance, while waiting for a job interview or to see the dentist, you may find that your reaction to the anxiety you feel is to bite your nails or to bounce your feet up and down. This serves the purpose of helping you to calm down and focus.

Stimming can also be a sign that someone is under-responsive to sensory stimuli and is seeking more sensory input.

So what's the problem with stimming?

This depends very much on your point of view. If your view is that stimming has a purpose, then you most likely won't have a problem with it. In fact, stopping someone from stimming can seem cruel; it is essentially stopping someone from helping to rebalance their over-stressed system.

However, there are many parents and teachers who prefer to stop a child from stimming. This can be for one of many reasons: sometimes the stim can be inappropriate in a public environment (e.g. touching themselves in places you'd really rather they wouldn't in public); some stims can be dangerous and risk a child's health and wellbeing; some people feel stimming marks the child out as 'different'; some feel they distract others in the class.

Should I stop my child from stimming?

Generally, my answer would be no. Go ahead and let them stim because this is a behaviour that serves a purpose. My only one proviso would be that if the stim is inappropriate or could hurt the person (or someone else), you should try to help them find a stim which will not be such a problem. One way to do this might be by writing a social story about it.

> If your view is that stimming has a purpose, then you most likely won't have a problem with it.

Support groups

Being a parent of a child with ASC can sometimes seem a lonely place. It is very easy to imagine that you're the first and only parent to go through what you're currently going through – the meltdowns, the struggles with funding, placements, meetings, snide looks and words from strangers. I could go on. But you are not the first. You also won't be the last. There will be thousands of others that have gone through the same or very similar struggles. And what's more, lots of them will have organised and set up support groups of various sorts. They're already out there, ready to share their accumulated wisdom and advice.

Where can I find a support group?

A good place to start is the internet. There are hundreds of support groups on social media. A quick search on Facebook or Twitter will furnish you with more than enough support group possibilities. In the UK, I'd really recommend searching for your local National Autistic Society support group (you'll be able to find your local branch by looking on the National Autistic Society website). You'll also find your local branch will probably have a Facebook group you can join immediately, and that will give you details of meetings, coffee mornings and support available and will put you in touch with other parents in your area who have children with ASC.

What can a support group do for me?

The answer to this question is that there is no single answer. A support group can do many things, from providing advice, information and support, to helping you build a friendship group of people who are going through similar experiences to you. Support groups often campaign and organise fundraising events. As with most things of this nature, the amount you get out of it is closely linked to the amount you put in. If you choose to dip in and out of a support group, you'll probably get the support or advice you need and not much else. If you decide to get really involved with helping out in the group, you'll probably find that you come away not just with support and advice, but a whole lot more beside.

CASE STUDY

Fran

The most amazing support group I know of is a group for parents of children with ASC, learning difficulties and challenging behaviours.

The Facebook page was set up following a conference in London – possibly the best £80 I've ever spent. I met parents like me: parents who were having a troubled time looking after their children whilst their children were physically violent towards them – the ultimate taboo.

Often we parents were told (by professionals!) that it was us at fault and our parenting 'made' our children violent. Having the forum to meet others, to share 'horror stories' without fear of judgement, to feel solidarity, to hear (from professionals who 'got it') that our children are wired differently and that this is not our fault, and to laugh at some bizarre remembrances, was a life-saver.

is for

Toileting

I can't hold it any longer. No, it's no use. I have to... talk about toileting.

Oh, that's better.

For a lot of children with ASC this isn't an issue, but for many (and also many who do not have ASC), toileting is a big issue. It is relatively common for children with ASC to take a little longer to toilet train.

Is my child ready?

Often, your child will give you hints that they are ready to try toilet training. Things to look out for are:

- Your child has become aware of when they need to go to the toilet.
- Your child is communicating that they need changing when they have a wet/soiled nappy.
- Your child shows discomfort at having a full nappy.
- Your child shows an interest in using the toilet or potty.
- Your child is becoming aware of when they have finished weeing or pooing in their nappy.

Toilet training

Ideally, you'll want to choose a time when there are few stresses, engagements and appointments to get started with toilet training. Many parents choose a school holiday for this, the summer holiday being ideal as it is longer and the weather is perfect for drying washing and for your child to be wearing less layers. However, you'll also be waiting for your child to show some indication that they are ready, as above.

Speak to nursery/school

As toilet training tends not to happen overnight but over a few months, there is a likelihood that some of the toilet training may be done by people other than you, in places other than the family home. To make sure that the process is similar in settings other than home, I'd recommend speaking to the setting or school which your child attends when starting to toilet train. Believe me, they will be only too pleased to help you get your child out of nappies and using the toilet independently. If you are using a potty or potty seat for your child, make sure you provide the school with similar and also provide a change of clothing in case of accidents. Talk to them about any routines which you and your child have developed around toilet training. The school may also have some suggestions of their own to help you.

Routine

As most children with ASC like routine and predictability, building a routine around toileting may be a good way for you to get started. To begin, you may like to change the nappies or trainer pants in the bathroom/toilets, so your child starts to make the link between toileting and the toilet. It would be a good idea to spend a while noting the times when your child often goes to the toilet in their nappy or pants. If you can establish some key times, you can then start to build the routine around using the potty or toilet at these times.

Visuals

Many people find that using visual aids is a good way to help their child understand the toileting process, to be able to follow the steps and be able to communicate their needs. A visual sequence near the toilet may help them to understand and follow the steps (i.e. trousers down, pants down, sit on the toilet, use the toilet, wipe, pants up, trousers up, flush). Make sure the sequence you use is the same as the one your child will be doing; so, if you are teaching your child to stand to pee, make sure you choose a visual sequence that shows this rather than sitting.

If your child is non-verbal or has delayed speech and language, you can use a signal, sign or symbol for them to communicate to you that they need to go to the toilet.

Persevere

To begin with, you will need to go through the process of going to the bathroom and following the visual sequence, without your child actually doing a wee or poo. This is common with all children and if you keep the experience positive – praising for following the steps – and persevere, you should find that eventually your child will start to go.

Rewards

Rewards and praise will give your child a reason to want to use the toilet and stick to the routine and sequence. You will probably know best what motivates your child, but it can be something as simple as verbal praise or a hug or something more involved such as a sticker chart.

Clothing

Make sure your child is dressed in clothes which they can easily manage themselves. Rather than poppers, buttons and buckles, go for elasticated waistbands and loose-fitting clothing.

Accidents

Accidents are inevitable in the process of toilet training. When they happen, take your child to the toilet (hopefully getting some of the wee in the toilet) and praise them for it. Try not to be cross (even if they just soiled the sofa) as this will introduce stress into the situation, which is likely to hinder your attempts at toilet training.

Night

Most children become mainly dry during the day before they toilet train for nighttime. Most of the same advice applies as for daytime. It's a good idea to establish a clear bedtime routine, taking your child to the toilet just before bed. It's also a good idea to avoid giving your child any fluid for an hour before bed. You may find that you also need to take them to the toilet once during the night, such as just before you go to bed yourself. You can get mattress protectors to stop the mattress from being damaged. Just as before, you should try to avoid seeming upset or annoyed if your child doesn't stay dry during the night, but praise them for following the routine.

The bowels

Some children with ASC have more difficulty with bowel movements, even after they have learned to wee in the toilet.

Squelch

Some children find the sensory sensation of having a filled nappy comforting. This can be because of the weight of the nappy, but also because of the feeling the contents of the nappy gives them. You can help them to get the sensory experience they are seeking in a more acceptable way, such as by giving them a cornflour and water mix (no, not in their nappy) or a weighted blanket or jacket.

Constipation

Constipation is a fairly common complaint of children with ASC. This can be scary for a child, as when they go to the toilet it can be painful. The cause might be to do with digestion, diet, or a fear of going to the toilet. If you are worried that your child is constipated, you could try explaining the process of digestion, so they understand what is happening. You could also try to introduce more fibre to their diet, which should help things move a little more smoothly. If you are still concerned, consult a medical professional.

Triad of impairments

The triad of impairments sounds like a really inclusive Chinese mafia movie. It's not though, or else it would have no place in this book. It is, in fact, a description of the three main areas where all people with ASC have difficulty. It was first described by Lorna Wing in 1979. More recently, diagnostic criteria also recognise sensory issues as a common feature of people on the autism spectrum.

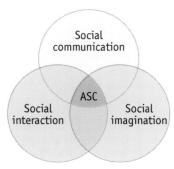

The Triad of Impairments

The three areas of the triad of impairments are social communication, social interaction and social imagination. They sound pretty similar. This is what they mean:

Social communication

This is the part of the triad which primarily deals with speech. Some (although not all) people with ASC have delays in their language skills. Difficulties with social communication can include not being able to process language or understand other non-verbal communication, such as body language, tone of voice and facial expressions. A common difficulty is not being able to follow complex instructions due to difficulties processing language. Many people with ASC need instructions broken down into smaller, more manageable chunks. It is also fairly common for people with ASC to take language very literally and therefore struggle to understand sarcasm, idioms, metaphors and similes. People with ASC often find it difficult to describe how they feel too.

Social interaction

This is the area which deals with forming and maintaining social relationships. This may cause difficulties in areas such as eye contact and invading personal space. People with ASC may struggle to pick up on cues that a listener is bored, tired or angry. They may also struggle to reciprocate in conversation, showing no interest in what the other person is saying. They may speak in a monotone, have difficulty regulating the level of their voice, or butt in during conversations or at inappropriate times. As these things can come across as rude, it often makes it very difficult for people with social interaction difficulties to socialise.

Social imagination

This is to do with being able to see the world from others' points of view. Social imagination allows us to understand and make predictions about the behaviour of others and to imagine things that are out of our own everyday routine. This can impact on people with ASC in several ways. They may find it difficult to understand that other people have different thoughts, feelings and experiences than their own. As a consequence, they might find social situations which involve reading the intentions of others difficult to deal with. It can also be difficult for people with ASC to make predictions about what might happen. Preparing for and coping with change can be challenging for people with ASC, which can make coping in new and unfamiliar situations extremely difficult and stressful for them. Sometimes people with ASC also have difficulty understanding the concept of danger.

Help is at hand

While there is no magic wand to make the triad of impairments disappear in a puff of smoke, there are many things you can do to help; for example, social stories and work on emotions, body language and facial expressions can greatly help children with ASC. For a fuller list of strategies that could help, see the section on speech and language therapy on page 145.

is for

Visual aids

Having a child with ASC, you are likely to come across visual aids of one sort or another. Whether it is a visual timetable, Picture Exchange Communication System (PECS), comic strip conversations or something else, visual communication has been found to work especially well for children with ASC.

Why visuals?

One defining aspect of ASC is difficulties with communication. This comes in many forms – some children may be non-verbal, some may have difficulties with reading non-verbal communication and others with their expressive or receptive language. Either way, visual aids are a good way of communicating information. For a start, if chosen well, they convey the message in a straightforward way, without room for misinterpretation. In addition, whereas the spoken word is gone as soon as the speaker has finished, a visual aid is a form of communication that can be referred to over and over again if a child is unsure of or forgets what it says. In some cases, a visual aid can prove to be less intrusive than the spoken word – for instance, showing a 'good sitting' card in a lesson can be done much more subtly than telling someone to sit up straight. A visual is often much less confrontational than the spoken word too, and for some children this can make a big difference. Visual supports are also usually portable and can be adapted and reused as required.

What types of visual aids might my child benefit from?

Visual timetable

These come in various forms. They can be helpful at home and at school in numerous ways including by providing routine, structure and predictability; preparing children for transitions; helping children take control over the tasks they do during the day and communicating in an unambiguous way.

A scale to monitor emotion levels

Again, these may come in many different forms and may be used for different purposes. They are often used to help children recognise how they are feeling and what an appropriate response to that feeling is. However, they can also be used to scale anything that might need monitoring and adjusting, such as the level of their voice.

Reward chart

Extrinsic rewards often work well for children with ASC. Reward charts, which can be designed to reflect the interests of the child, are a great visual way of tracking progress and work well as an incentive.

Facial expressions cards

Children with ASC often find difficulty with non-verbal communication such as facial expressions and emotions. Practising recognising them with photograph or symbol cards can help.

Now/next cards

This is a simple chart with two boxes – one for 'now' and one for 'next' – which can be used to ease transitions, or as a simpler form of visual timetable.

PECS

This is a system which works well for children with little or no language, whereby they use simple symbols to communicate their needs.

Task analysis charts

These help to break complicated tasks into simple steps, using visuals and sometimes simple instructions. They can be used for anything from doing school work to getting dressed, from boiling an egg to building a Lego model.

Visual organisers

These are helpful ways of organising information that a child might need to complete their work. They include things such as mind maps, story maps, comic strips and word walls.

Social stories

Social stories help to explain tricky social situations. Because they're often written down and printed out, they can be taken out and used as often as needed, thus making them more effective than a verbal explanation of the social situation. See page 136 for more information.

Comic strip conversations

Comic strip conversations set out a social scenario which has caused a difficulty or misunderstanding. Simple visuals (usually stick people) are usually used. See page 30 for more information.

Choice boards

Choice boards are a visual way to offer a simple choice. Just present a choice – perhaps two activities – using symbols on the board, so your child can choose between them.

Oops cards

Oops cards are a simple device to help children anticipate and prepare for a change in routine. The oops card is simply placed on the visual timetable at the point where a change has been made. (See page 111 for more details.)

Glossary

of acronyms

ADOS **Autism Diagnosing Observation Schedule**
This is the set of tasks and assessments used to diagnose autism. In the case of children, this will be the assessment which happens when your child is seen by the examiner.

AS **Asperger syndrome**
AS is one of the presentations of autism. Those with AS have average or above-average intelligence, but have difficulty with social understanding.

ASC **Autism spectrum condition**
This is the catch-all diagnosis for all of the different presentations of autism.

ASD **Autism spectrum disorder**
It is the same as ASC, autism, the spectrum etc.

CAMHS **Child and Adolescent Mental Health Services**
This is the service most children will be referred to for an assessment of autism.

CBT **Cognitive behavioural therapy**
This is a type of therapy that helps the patient to view their problems more positively and break them down into smaller, more manageable chunks.

EHCP   **Education, Health and Care Plan**

This is a legal document which can be applied for when a child with SEN has higher needs. The EHCP sets out provision and often comes with funding attached.

ELSA   **Emotional Literacy Support Assistant**

Many schools have ELSAs who work with children to identify, understand and deal with their emotions.

EP   **Educational psychologist**

Educational psychologists help children with a range of issues which may affect their learning, including social skills.

IEP   **Individual Education Plan**

This is a document that a school produces to show the targets and interventions that young people with SEN receive. They are usually written and reviewed two or three times a year. It may be referred to by other names, such as SEN Support Plan.

M-CHAT   **Modified Checklist for Autism in Toddlers**

This is an online quiz which you can take to give some indication as to whether your child may have autism.

ODD   **Oppositional defiance disorder**

A condition which is categorised by negative and disruptive behaviour, especially towards authority figures.

OT   **Occupational therapy**

Occupational therapy is used to help people whose health stops them from being able to do the things they want or need to do. It is often used to help children with sensory needs and to improve motor skills..

PDA   **Pathological demand avoidance**

This is a behavioural profile which some children with autism may have. It is characterised by the child seeking to avoid all demands placed on them. PDA is not recognised as a diagnosis of its own at present.

PDD   **Pervasive developmental disorder**

PDD refers to a category of disorders, rather than a specific diagnosis. There are five disorders in this category; four of them are on the autism spectrum and the other is Rett Syndrome.

PDD-NOS **Pervasive developmental disorder – not otherwise specified**

This is one of the autism spectrum disorders, which is sometimes called atypical autism. It is not used any more; instead, a child is likely to receive a diagnosis of ASC.

PECS **Picture Exchange Communication System**

This is a communication system which many people with ASC use. It uses clear picture symbols as a means of communication.

SALT **Speech and language therapy**

Most children with autism will work with speech and language therapy at some point. It can help with expressive and receptive language, active listening, and the social aspects of language and communication.

SEN **Special educational needs**

Sometimes also referred to as SEND (the D standing for Disability).

SENCo **Special Educational Needs Coordinator**

This is the person within a school who has responsibility for ensuring appropriate provision for SEN pupils. By law every school must have a SENCo.

SPD **Sensory Processing Disorder**

This is a neurological condition where the brain finds it difficult to process information from the senses. This can manifest in being either over- or under- sensitive to one or more sense.

Index

Notes